Vorwort

Durch die zunehmende Globalisierung, die Entwicklung der Europäischen Union und ihre Erweiterung sowie die Internationalisierung der Märkte ist der Kontakt mit Menschen aus dem Ausland immer intensiver geworden. Handel und Industrie sind zu einem großen Teil abhängig vom Export ins Ausland. Seit Jahrhunderten bestehen intensive Kontakte mit Menschen aus dem Ausland. In Deutschland wohnen zudem ungefähr 6,7 Millionen Ausländer. Im Rahmen der Schul- und Ausbildung ist daher der Erwerb einer Fremdsprache von großer Bedeutung. Im Besonderen sind Kenntnisse der englischen Sprache als Handelssprache und Mittel zur weltweiten Verständigung unverzichtbar.

Auch für Menschen im Sicherheitsgewerbe, ist es von Bedeutung, dass sie sich in Englisch gut ausdrücken können. Die Zahl englischsprachiger Fachausdrücke wächst stetig; bereits jetzt sind Begriffe wie 'security awareness', 'clean desk' und 'slow woop' im Sicherheitsgewerbe gebräuchlich.

Sicherheitsfachkräfte müssen in englischer Sprache veröffentlichten Funktionsanleitungen und -anweisungen technische Informationen entnehmen können. Ferner können sich im Veranstaltungs- und Objektschutz Situationen ergeben, bei denen in englischer Sprache kommuniziert werden muss.

In diesem Buch erwerben Sie Basiskenntnisse und Grundfertigkeiten der englischen Sprache, im Wesentlichen zur verbalen Kommunikation, mit deren Hilfe eine angemessene Verständigung in der Fremdsprache ermöglicht wird.

In den Kapiteln dieses Buches werden Situationen aus Ihrem beruflichen Handlungsfeld aufgegriffen. Zu jeder Situation gehören Übungen, für die gegebenenfalls zu Übungszwecken die zugehörige CD-ROM verwendet wird. In einem solchen Fall findet sich folgendes Symbol neben der Übung:

Natürlich werden vorwiegend englische Ausdrücke verwendet. Ein Kapitel wird daher als 'Unit' bezeichnet, eine Situation als 'event' und eine dazugehörige Übung als 'task'.

Track

Auf Vokabeln, die erforderlich sind, um die englischen Texte zu verstehen, wird am Textrand verwiesen. Zur Vertiefung der notwendigsten Basiskenntnisse und ‑fertigkeiten bietet das letzte Kapitel einen Überblick über die englische Grammatik.
Obwohl die Aufgaben- und Servicebereiche im Sicherheitsdienstleistungsgewerbe im In- und Ausland nahezu identisch sind, existieren große Unterschiede in der Ausbildung und in den Qualifizierungsmaßnahmen der Mitarbeiter.

Der häufig in der englischsprachigen Fachliteratur verwendete Begriff „security officer" ist in Deutschland am ehesten der „geprüften Schutz- und Sicherheitskraft" zuzuordnen und daher mit der allgemeinen Bezeichnung für „Sicherheitskraft" gleichzusetzen.
Bei dem in Deutschland für das Sicherheitsgewerbe eingeführten Berufsbild der ‚Fachkraft für Schutz und Sicherheit' handelt es sich um eine 3-jährige berufliche Erstausbildung mit einer bundesweit einheitlich anerkannten Ausbildungsordnung. Die ‚Fachkraft für Schutz und Sicherheit' erwirbt Kenntnisse, die sie vor allem im analytischen und kaufmännischen Bereich gegenüber einer Sicherheitskraft höher qualifiziert. Aus diesem Grund ist diese Berufsbezeichnung mit ‚safety and security specialist' zu übersetzen.

Die Verfasserin und die Herausgeber möchten an dieser Stelle all denen danken, die mit Anregungen, Kommentaren, Bild- und Textmaterial oder auf andere Weise zum Entstehen von ‚Englisch für Sicherheitskräfte' beigetragen haben.
Unser besonderer Dank gilt:

Willem Jurry (Übungen)
Peter Saes (Übungen und Audio-CD Aufnahmen)

Sue Westlake
Barbara Jacobs
Björn Stapper
AVG Köln mbH, Köln
Berufskolleg West der Stadt Essen, Essen
B.E.S.T. Veranstaltungsdienste GmbH, Berlin
Emden Marketing und Tourismus GmbH, Emden
FC Gelsenkirchen-Schalke 04 e.V., Gelsenkirchen
Flughafen Düsseldorf International, Düsseldorf
Fraport AG, Frankfurt
Gloria GmbH, Wadersloh
Goldschmidt GmbH, Essen
HERTHA BSC mbH KG aA, Berlin
Knoblich-Security GmbH, Köln
Kötter GmbH & Co. KG, Essen
MESSE ESSEN GmbH, Essen
Minimax GmbH & Co. KG, Bad Oldesloe
MS-SECURITY GUARD e. K., Essen
Olympiastadion Berlin GmbH, Berlin
SafetyConsult® Objekt- und Sicherheitskennzeichnung GmbH, Kelkheim
Securitas Holding GmbH, Düsseldorf
Sicherheitsdienste Delshad-Jooposht GmbH, Dinslaken
VSU Wachdienst Rhein-Ruhr GmbH, Bochum
Wachdienst Bremen GmbH, Gelsenkirchen
WE SECURE & PROTECT Ltd.& Co. KG, Halle (Westf.)

Andrea Metschke

02//

Tasks of a safety and security specialist, crimes and punishments

In diesem Teil lernen Sie englische Begriffe und Ausdrücke aus dem Bereich des Sicherheitswesens kennen.
Sie werden in englischer Sprache mit den Aufgaben einer Schutz- und Sicherheitskraft vertraut gemacht und erlernen Vokabeln von Straftaten und Maßnahmen, mit denen Sie in Ihrem beruflichen Handlungsfeld konfrontiert werden könnten.

A safety and security specialist

A safety and security specialist's job is to make sure that buildings, valuables or people are safe and secure. Many jobs involve dealing with people a lot of the time. Others are more technical, working with the latest technology in security systems. To do this job, people need to be:
*   mature, responsible and honest
*   healthy and physically fit
*   able to use their initiative and make quick decisions.
Safety and security specialists often work long hours and many do quite a bit of overtime. The work may be in the day or at night, and shift work is very common. There are many different kinds of places where safety and security specialists work - indoors or outdoors.

safety and security specialist*	Fachkraft für Schutz- und Sicherheit
valuables	Wertgegenstände, Wertsachen
safe	sicher (außer Gefahr)
secure	sicher, (vor Angriffen)
to involve	einbeziehen, mit sich bringen
mature	reif
responsible	verantwortungsbewusst, zuverlässig
honest	ehrlich
decision	Entscheidung
overtime	Überstunden
shift work	Schichtarbeit

*safty und security specialist ist die englische Bezeichnung für den deutschen Ausbildungsberuf "Fachkraft für Schutz und Sicherheit". Der im englischen Sprachraum gebräuchliche allgemeine Begriff für Sicherheitspersonal ist "security officer".

previous	früher, vorherig
experience	Erfahrung
prison	Gefängnis
armed forces	Streitkräfte
applicant	Bewerber
skill	Fertigkeit, Geschick
building site	Baustelle
task	Aufgabe

Some people move into security work when they are a bit older, and it can help a lot to have previous work experience, especially in the police, fire or prison services or the armed forces. Exam passes are not always needed, but applicants must be able to read and write. They will sometimes get extra training to learn new skills such as dog handling or using new technology.

Safety and security specialists can work in all kinds of large organisations, from hotels, hospitals, factories and offices to building sites, colleges, shopping centres, airports and ships. Growing numbers of safety and security specialists are needed all over the country.

Task 1

Read the text on the safety and security specialist and make a list of his tasks.

1. ....

2. ....

3. ....

4. ....

5. ....

6. ....

7. ....

8. ....

9. ....

10. ....

Task 2

Match the English (1-23) with the German (a-w) expressions on crime.
One has already been done for you.

1. armed robbery	a. Industriespionage
2. assault	b. Vergewaltigung
3. burglary	c. Drogenkonsum
4. computer crime	d. Diebstahl
5. credit card fraud	e. Mord
6. drug-taking	f. bewaffneter Raubüberfall
7. drug-trafficking	g. Entführung
8. drunk driving	h. Schmuggeln
9. hijacking	i. Mobbing
10. industrial espionage	j. Steuerhinterziehung
11. kidnapping	k. Kreditkartenbetrug
12. manslaughter	l. Einbruch
13. mugging	m. (Flugzeug-, Bus-) Entführung
14. murder	n. Ladendiebstahl
15. forgery	o. Totschlag
16. arson	p. Trunkenheit am Steuer
17. rape	q. Vandalismus
18. shoplifting	r. Straßenraub
19. smuggling	s. (tätlicher) Angriff
20. theft	t. Drogenhandel
21. vandalism	u. Computerkriminalität
22. tax evasion	v. Brandstiftung
23. mobbing	w. Fälschung

1	2	3	4	5	6	7	8	9	10	11	12	13	14	15	16	17	18	19	20	21	22	23
f																						

9

warning	Verwarnung, Warnung
community service	sozialer Dienst
fine	Buß-, Verwarnungsgeld, Geldstrafe
suspended	zur Bewährung ausgesetzt
sentence	Urteil, Strafe, Strafmaß
offender	Täter, Rechtsbrecher
probation	Bewährung
detention centre	Jugendstrafanstalt
verdict	Urteil
guilty	schuldig
breach	Verstoß, Übertretung

Task 3

Decide on a punishment for each of these crimes and form meaningful sentences. One has already been done for you.

1. A drug dealer with no criminal record so far

2. Teenagers who have shoplifted for the first time

3. A 16-year old murderer of two children

4. A person who committed computer crime

5. In case of manslaughter

6. A person who killed someone while drunk-driving

7. For a minor breach of the law

a. the court should impose a fine.

b. should be sentenced to a detention centre.

c. the court should require the offender to do community service.

d. the court should announce a verdict of guilty.

e. should be given a suspended prison sentence.

f. should not be let off with a warning.

g. should be put on probation for a certain period.

1 - g
2 -
3 -
4 -
5 -
6 -
7 -

Task 4

Find 12 types of crime and punishments in the word square (across and down)

Crossword

C	R	I	M	E	T	C	U	N	J	A	S	E	B	T	G
X	E	E	W	Q	K	R	X	C	Z	D	G	I	U	X	T
B	A	R	R	A	P	E	U	N	U	R	D	E	R	O	U
J	S	W	P	T	M	D	H	Z	I	U	N	Z	G	P	Z
O	S	H	O	P	L	I	F	T	I	N	G	G	L	A	B
P	A	Q	T	Q	P	T	E	J	A	K	E	R	A	I	T
S	U	A	H	S	A	C	K	K	K	D	R	B	R	J	A
A	L	S	J	E	D	A	L	A	M	R	T	P	Y	G	X
W	T	S	K	F	V	R	P	O	J	I	Z	A	Q	T	E
T	D	F	W	G	B	D	Q	E	P	V	U	S	P	X	V
Z	C	U	T	H	E	F	T	R	A	I	N	F	D	E	A
N	F	H	Z	J	N	R	J	G	K	N	B	M	E	W	S
I	Z	I	N	J	K	A	C	M	U	G	G	I	N	G	I
K	H	O	U	O	L	U	E	R	G	T	R	R	O	M	O
L	K	L	M	K	I	D	N	A	P	P	I	N	G	Z	N

10

03//

At the gate and on patrol

In diesem Teil machen Sie sich mit Fragen und Problemen vertraut, die Ihnen beim Empfangs- und Pfortendienst mit englischsprachigen Kunden oder Besuchern begegnen können. Viele Menschen im Sicherheitswesen arbeiten in diesen Bereichen, aber auch wenn Sie in anderen Aufgabengebieten tätig sind, können Ihnen die Hilfestellungen in englischer Sprache in vielen Situationen nützlich sein.

event	Ereignis, Veranstaltung
kind	Art, Sorte
security	Sicherheit
staff	Belegschaft, Personal
travellers	Reisende
to create	kreieren, gestalten
atmosphere	Atmosphäre
to feel comfortable	sich wohl fühlen
safety	Sicherheit
airport	Flughafen
detached to	angeschlossen
tighter	strenger, straffer
measures	Maßnahmen
to be on duty	Dienst haben
to be on surveillance	patrouillieren, einen Rundgang machen
premises	Gelände, Gebäude

Event

People need all kind of information. Security personnel help them out. They answer questions, show the way and give advice. They are there to assist travellers and thus help to create a nicer atmosphere in which people feel more comfortable and safer at the airport.

Persons involved

Andrea
Martina
Peter
Christine
Stefan
Thorsten
Corinna

} They are security staff detached to a unit at Düsseldorf Airport. Because of tighter safety measures personnel from the federal police (Bundespolizei) are on duty at the information desk near the Düsseldorf shopping centre or on surveillance on the premises.

Task 1

Listen to the conversation and draw a circle around the right answer. People talking to Andrea are looking for:

Track 01

the stationery department	Mr./Mrs. 1,2,3
the counter for tickets	Mr./Mrs. 1,2,3
the electrical department	Mr./Mrs. 1,2,3

conversation	Gespräch
to draw	zeichnen
department	Abteilung
stationery	Schreibwaren
counter	Tresen

11

Task 2

Track 01

Play task 1 again.
Who says what? Tick the appropriate box.

to tick	ankreuzen
appropriate	geeignet
to wonder	sich fragen
tax free	steuerfrei
base	Stützpunkt
army	Heer, Bundeswehr

Andrea	Client

- Excuse me.
- Yes, that's right.
- Certainly, sir.
- Thank you very much indeed.
- Can I help you, madam?
- Could you tell me where I...
- It's very easy to find.
- I wonder if you could tell me...
- It's a pleasure.

Task 3

What does Andrea think when she says the following? Match the numbers and letters. The first one has already been done for you.

1. Certainly, sir.
2. Why don't you try the electrical department?
3. It's very easy to find.
4. It's downstairs in the basement.
5. I don't understand.
6. That's right.
7. You'll find the counter just there.
8. It's a pleasure.

a. Was meinen Sie?
b. Das ist richtig.
c. Aber natürlich.
d. Da können Sie den Tresen finden.
e. Das ist sehr leicht zu finden.
f. Gerne. Zu Ihren Diensten.
g. Sie sollten es in der Elektroabteilung versuchen.
h. Das befindet sich unten im Untergeschoss.

1	2	3	4	5	6	7	8
c							

Task 4

Track 02

Peter is about to show someone the way but..........
A person comes to Peter with some papers in his hand and puts them on the desk.

12

Listen to and then read the following conversation. Then practise and switch roles.

to practise	üben
sheet	Blatt
to be embarrassed	verlegen sein
marvellous	großartig

...Oh, er could you photocopy this sheet?

Pardon?

Could you make a photocopy of this, please?

Oh, I see. Certainly. How many copies would you like to have?

One will do.

Just a moment, please... Here you are.

Marvellous. Thank you.

This way please.

Don't be embarrassed.......

Eines der schlimmsten Dinge, die passieren können, ist, dass Sie nicht verstehen oder begreifen, was jemand sagt. Das ist peinlich für Ihr Gegenüber und für Sie.
Sie müssen in so einem Fall erst deutlich machen, dass Sie nichts verstanden haben, zum Beispiel durch ein ‚Pardon?'. Sie können dann erwarten, dass die Frage oder der Satz wiederholt wird. Meist haben Muttersprachler viel Verständnis für diese Situation und sprechen dann langsamer oder versuchen es auf eine andere Weise zu formulieren.
Wenn es wieder nicht gelingt, können Sie wieder mit einem ‚Pardon?' reagieren oder freundlich darum bitten, etwas langsamer zu sprechen: ‚Could you speak more slowly, please?'. Wenn es dann immer noch nicht klappt, sollte eine dritte Person hinzugezogen werden. Zum Beispiel so: 'I am sorry, I'll call the supervisor.' Es gibt noch andere Tricks. Aber zu denen kommen wir später.
Verstehen Sie Ihr Gegenüber nachdem Sie ihn gebeten haben, langsamer zu sprechen, können Sie zum Beispiel reagieren mit ‚Oh, I see.'

13

Task 5

Track 03

Listen to the following role play.

to perforate	perforieren
to punch	lochen
hole	Loch

Excuse me, where can I find the nearest cash desk?

Pardon?

Where do I pay?

Oh, I see. It's over there, near the exit.

Now play this dialogue. Switch roles.

Task 6

Track 04

Now try the same conversation with these questions and answers, when you're finished, switch roles:

Could you print this copy on red paper?

Pardon?

Could you make a photocopy of this on red paper, please?

Oh, I see. Yes, of course. How many copies would you like?

One will do. Could you also perforate it for me?

Could you repeat that, please?

Erm, could you also punch them for me, please?

Oh, now I see, you want me to punch holes in it, isn't it?

Yes, please.

Here they are.

Thanks.

You're welcome.

14

Task 7

You work at the reception desk. There are some people who ask you for information. You find it difficult to understand them. So you try again.
Look at the 'flow chart'. It offers you different ways of saying things. Make your choice from each box.
Play these dialogues with a partner. Then switch roles.

Where can I find the washroom, please?
Could you tell me where the cash desk is, please?
Where can I find the cloakroom?
Where can I leave my valuables?

- Pardon?

Where can I wash my hands?
Where's the cash desk?
Where's the cloakroom?
Where can I leave my valuables?

- Could you speak more slowly, please?

Where is the toilet, please?
Where can I pay?
Where can I hang my coat?
Do you have a safe so I can give you this briefcase
with important papers?

- I'm sorry, I'll ask the supervisor.
- Oh, I see. Yes, of course. It's over there,
  near the swingdoors.

flow chart	Flussdiagramm
choice	Wahl
dialogue	Dialog
cash desk	Kasse
exit	Ausgang
to repeat	wiederholen
essential	wesentlich
message	Nachricht
to be able to	können
to indicate	anzeigen, -deuten
asterisk	Sternchen
to highlight	hervorheben, mit Leuchtstift markieren
pronunciation	Aussprache
sound	Laut, Klang
mistake	Fehler

Example:

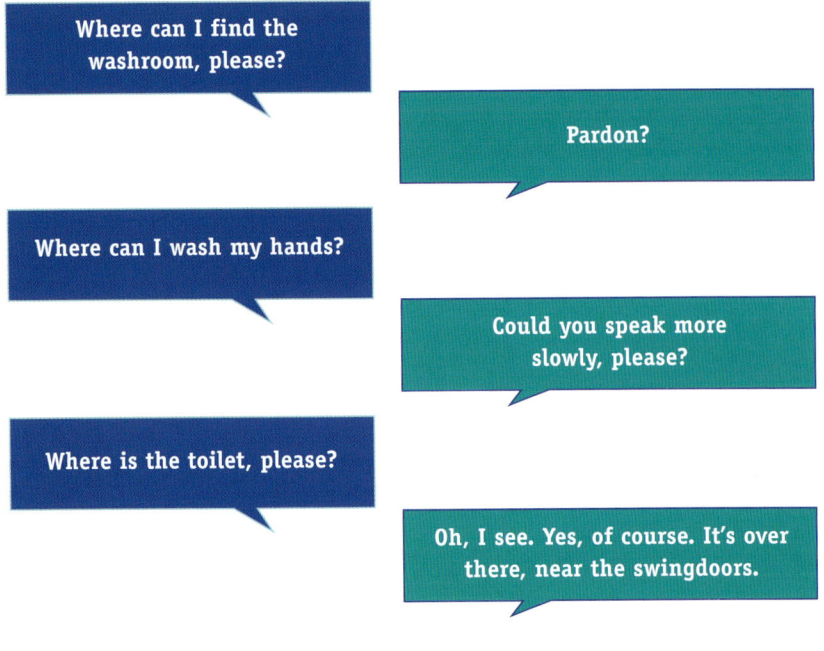

Task 8

Track 05

The alphabet is very important. It is essential in communication. You need the alphabet to pass messages, either written or spoken. So you must be able to spell the alphabet correctly. Pay extra attention to letters indicated with an asterisk. Listen and practise.

		D			D			D
*	A	[äi]	**	J	[dschäi]	*	S	[eß]
	B	[bih]		K	[käi]		T	[tih]
	C	[ßie]		L	[el]		U	[juh]
	D	[dih]		M	[em]		V	[vih]
*	E	[ih]		N	[en]	*	W	[dabljuh]
	F	[ef]		O	[ou]		X	[äks]
*	G	[dschih]		P	[pih]	*	Y	[wai]
*	H	[äitsch]		Q	[kjuh]	*	Z	[sed]
*	I	[ai]		R	[ah]	*	Z	US: [sih]
				R	US: [ahr]			

Now work in pairs:

One person practises the ABC aloud. The other checks the pronunciation with the help of the book. Any mistakes?
Now switch roles.

16

Pronunciation game:

Think about how the following letters of the English alphabet are pronounced.
Highlight the word that has the same sound as the letter of the alphabet.

The first one is an example:

A	star	stay
B	bay	bee
E	see	say
G	kay	key
H	age	ouch
I	me	my
K	bug	bay
L	bell	bill
O	no	new
Q	new	near
R	are	ear
T	tea	tray
U	Jane	June
V	kay	key
X	next	near
Y	life	leave
Z(US)	key	bed
Z(GB)	key	bed

Task 9

Christine is on surveillance. She is making her rounds in the Airport Hotel. On her way she is addressed by some people.

You are on duty at the information desk of the hotel. A visitor wants to get some information.

Track 06

to be addressed	angesprochen werden
visitor	Besucher

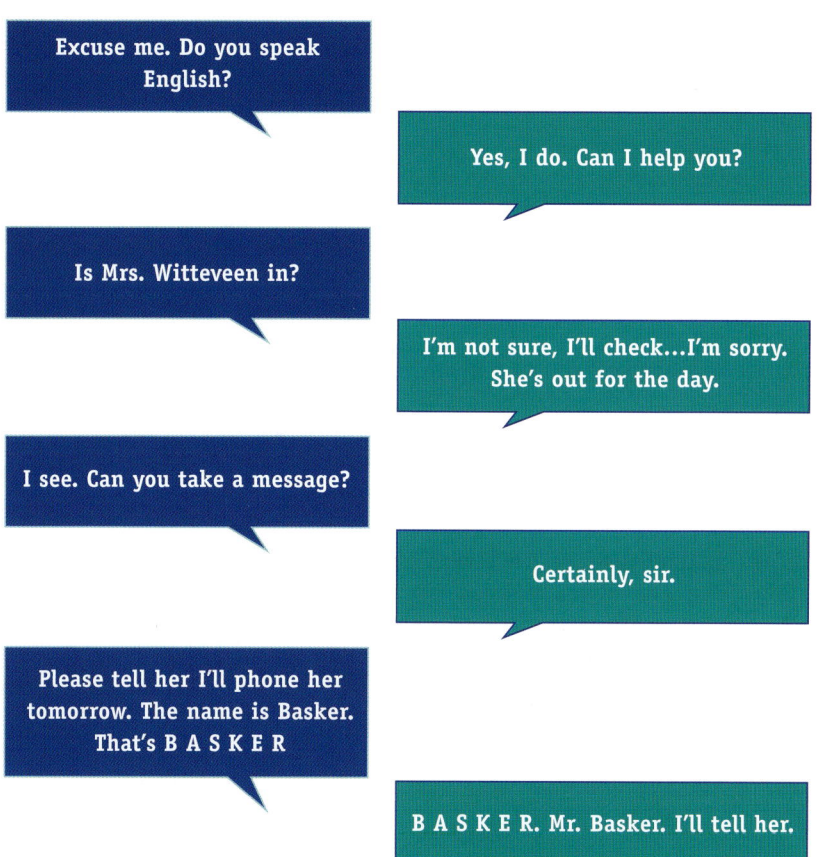

Excuse me. Do you speak English?

Yes, I do. Can I help you?

Is Mrs. Witteveen in?

I'm not sure, I'll check...I'm sorry. She's out for the day.

I see. Can you take a message?

Certainly, sir.

Please tell her I'll phone her tomorrow. The name is Basker. That's B A S K E R

B A S K E R. Mr. Basker. I'll tell her.

17

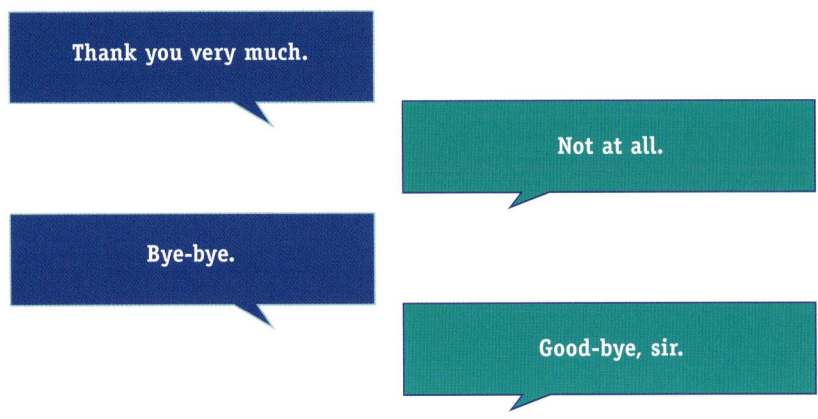

Task 10

Track 07

Now listen to four short conversations in the same hotel.
Please write down the names of these people (in the right order)

1. Mr./Mrs..................................
2. Mr./Mrs..................................
3. Mr./Mrs..................................
4. Mr./Mrs..................................

Telephone game:
Form groups of three or more people. You are on the telephone and somebody asks you to spell out your name. Spell out your own first name, in the same way as in the example. The others in the group check if it is done right. Then switch.

My first name is Peter, P-E-T-E-R; Peter.
Now spell out your last name, in the same way as in the example. The others in the group check if it is done right. Then switch.
My last name is Kirstein, I spell, K-I-R-S-T-E-I-N; Kirstein.

More tasks:

A. Read aloud and pronounce the letters in English.

B. Replace the underlined letters by words and names from the alphabetical list below and also fill in the gaps. Watch out! There are more words than underlined letters.

1. I C a honeyB on that flower.
2. Do you C that Jbird in that tree.
3. I'm very fond of MinM's rapmusic. M&Ms have a chocolate coating.
4. Heike Makatsch was a famous VJ, didn't she work for MTV?
5. K's Choice is a popular Belgian pop group. Is the name of the lead singer K?
6. DJs often replace live bands!
7. J.F. Kennedy's first names were..............
8. AA stands for.......
9. Lmore is a beautiful name. Do U love it 2?
10. I'm very Qrious about my test results.
11. I go to the bathroom for a P.
12. The USA won many gold medals . The name stands for the..............
13. Would you like some more T?
14. L Al is an Israeli airline.

to check	kontrollieren
example	Beispiel
to learn by heart	auswendig lernen
family name	Nachname
first name	Vorname
last name	Nachname
underlined	unterstrichen
exercise	Übung
coating	Schicht, Überzug
bathroom	Badezimmer
to pee	pinkeln
airplane	Flugzeug
curious	neugierig
marine	Marinesoldat
jaybird	Eichelhäher
age	Alter
airline	Fluggesellschaft

18

15.   <u>Y</u> is U2 so popular?
16.   My father is an <u>X</u>-Marine.
17.   <u>H</u> sounds like age.
18.   The Fanta <u>4</u> belong to Germany's <u>VIP</u>s.
19.   Do you think the <u>NFL</u> have it on DVD or <u>CD</u>-ROM?
20.   This is the <u>Nd</u> of the exercise.

Words:	Names:
bee	Against Alcohol
compact disk	American Airlines
curious	Against
disk jockey	El Al
electronic	Elmore
end	Eminem
ex-marine	John Fitzgerald
extra	Josua Fred
four	Kay
jaybird	Music Television
pee	National Football League
see	(United States)
tea	United States of America
thee	Very Important Person
tool	
video jockey	
why	
you	

Task 11

Track 08

Today is November 22nd. The time is 10.30. Stefan is at the reception desk and a visitor, Mr. Crafter, has a meeting in the hotel. Listen to the conversation. Work in pairs. Take turns.

Thorsten has the order to receive visitors at a security fair in Essen. He also has to supply them with a badge with their name on it.
Listen to the conversation. Work in pairs. Take turns.

meeting	Besprechung, Konferenz
to take turns	sich abwechseln
to receive	empfangen
to supply	versorgen
badge	Namensschild

> **Good-morning. My name is Crafter. Do you speak English?**

> **I do, sir. Can I help you?**

> **I'd like to see Mr. Willemse. I have a meeting with him at 10.30.**

> **I see. I'll tell Mr. Willemse that you are here. What was your name again, please, sir?**

> **Crafter. C-R-A-F-T-E-R.**

Crafter. Could you please fill in this form, Mr. Crafter?

OK... What date is it today?

November 22nd. Thank you sir. And here is your badge. Mr. Willemse will be down in a minute to show you upstairs.

Task 12

Track 09

Have a look at the clock. What time is it? Listen and practise.

10 nach 10	ten minutes past ten	10 past 10
Viertel nach 10	a quarter past ten	
5 vor halb 11	twenty-five minutes past ten	25 past 10
Halb 11	half past ten	
20 vor 11	twenty minutes to eleven	20 to 11
Viertel vor 11	a quarter to eleven	
11 Uhr	11 o'clock	

Pay extra attention to:

Viertel nach 10	ten fifteen	10.15 h*
Halb 11	ten thirty	10.30 h
Viertel vor 11	ten forty-five	10.45 h
11 Uhr	eleven	11.00 h

to pay attention to   beachten

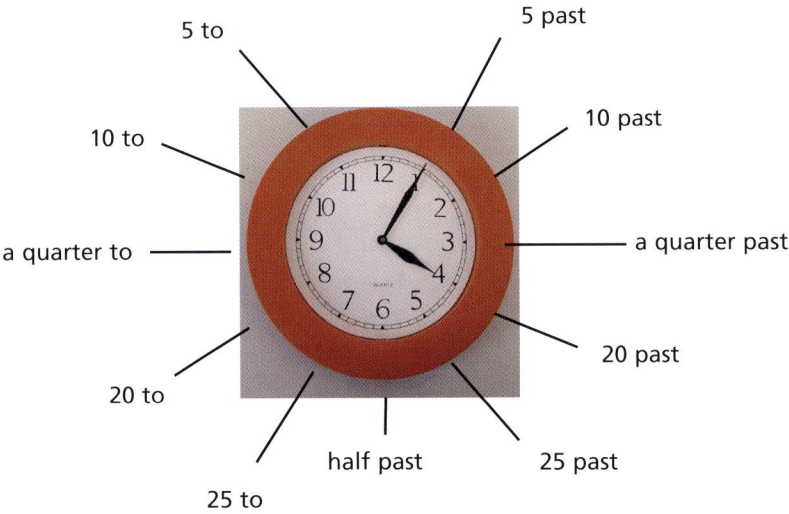

* h ist die internationale Abkürzung für 'Stunde' - dies wird auch oft weggelassen

Task 13

Listen to the hours of the clock. Are the hours indicated the correct ones? If so, please put in a mark.

1 ☐   2 ☐   3 ☐   4 ☐   5 ☐

6 ☐   7 ☐   8 ☐   9 ☐   10 ☐

Task 14

Stefan will see more people today. Listen to the conversations and write down the names and hours.

Track 11

name	hours
1. Mr. Johnson	9.30
2.	
3.	
4.	

Task 15

Thinking of time it is not only the clock that matters. There are the days of the weeks and the months making up the year. Now you will get to know the names of the twelve months. Listen carefully and then repeat.

Track 12

Januar	January
Februar	February
März	March
April	April
Mai	May
Juni	June
Juli	July
August	August
September	September
Oktober	October
November	November
Dezember	December

Bei Datumsangaben gebraucht man im Englischen die Ordnungszahlen. Das bedeutet, man sagt: Der erste Januar, der einunddreißigste August, der vierzehnte Juli...
Es gibt Unterschiede zwischen der Schreibweise und der Aussprache von Datumsangaben. Außerdem gibt es Unterschiede zwischen der amerikanischen und britischen Datumsangabe.
Als Mr. Crafter nach dem Datum fragte, sagte Thorsten: ‚*November the twenty-second*.' Dies ist die amerikanische Variante. Er hätte auch sagen können: ‚*The twenty-second of November*.' (British English)
In seiner Formulierungsweise hätte Mr. Crafter es dann so eingetragen: November 22 oder 22 November.*

* die Monate beginnen im Englischen **immer** mit einem Großbuchstaben.

Bitte beachten Sie nur Folgendes:

first, second, third
eleventh, twelfth, thirteenth
twenty-first, twenty-second
twenty-third, thirty-first usw.

Task 16

Track 13

Here is the calendar of the month of January. Listen to the days of the weeks. Find the days you hear and tick the appropriate box.

January						
Monday		2	9	16	23	30
Tuesday		3	10	17	24	31
Wednesday		4	11	18	25	
Thursday		5	12	19	26	
Friday		6	13	20	27	
Saturday		7	14	21	28	
Sunday	1	8	15	22	29	

Task 17

Here is the calendar of the whole year. Find the days you hear and tick the appropriate box. If you work it out correctly, a drawing will show up.

Track 14

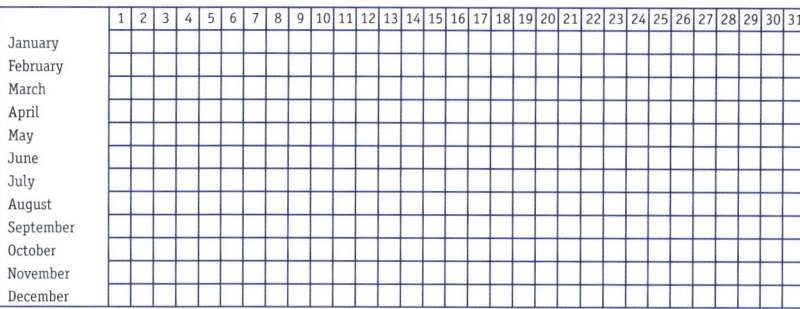

	1	2	3	4	5	6	7	8	9	10	11	12	13	14	15	16	17	18	19	20	21	22	23	24	25	26	27	28	29	30	31
January																															
February																															
March																															
April																															
May																															
June																															
July																															
August																															
September																															
October																															
November																															
December																															

Task 18

Crossword puzzle:

	1	2	3	4	5	6	7	8	9	10	11	12	13	14	15	16	17
2																	
3																	
4																	
5																	
6																	
7																	
8																	
9																	
10																	
11																	
12																	
13																	
14																	

Down:
6 Month when two aeroplanes flew into the WTC in New York.
8 On the first day of this month many people light fireworks.
12 In this month many birds lay an egg.
13 Some people already have summer holidays, others don't.
14 This month sounds like military walking or playing military music.
17 At first it was the 8th month, now it's the 10th month.

Across:
5 Most busy holiday month.
6 The fourth month of the year.
7 Usually the coldest month of the year, in which you send the hottest postcard to a secret lover.
10 This month is named after a Roman emperor and later became the eights month.
11 Month of the start of next year's Carnival.
13 Christmas month and the month of New Year's Eve.

fireworks	Feuerwerk
holiday	Ferien
emperor	Kaiser
New Year's Eve	Silvesterabend

23

Task 19

Work in pairs.

> When is your birthday?
> When is Christmas Day?
> What date is today?
> What date was yesterday?
> What date is tomorrow?
> When is your best friend's birthday?

Make sentences. Take turns.

> My birthday is...........................
> Christmas Day is....................
> ....
> ....
> ....
> ....

Task 20

Track 15

When you count, you use figures. Figures make numbers. You are going to practise them. Listen and repeat. Pay close attention to figures ending in -/teen and -/ty like in thirteen (13) and thirty (30).

number	Zahl
to count	zählen
to repeat	wiederholen
to pronounce	aussprechen
difference	Unterschied
blank	unausgefüllt
recipe	Rezept
introduction	Einleitung
at least	mindestens
magazine	Zeitschrift

1	2	3	4	5	6	7	8	9	10
11	12	13	14	15	16	17	18	19	20
21	22	23	24	25	26	27	28	29	30
40	50	60	70	80	90	100			
41	52	63	74	85	96	107	117	128	139

Task 21

Track 16

Find out the differences between these figures/ numbers.

52	25	13	30	18	80
36	63	14	40	19	90
48	84	15	50		
69	96	16	60		
74	47	17	70		

Task 22

Track 17

Listen and tick the appropriate box if the number is correct.

25	30	15	67	8	0	80	114	25	14	70	13

Task 23

Listen and write down the numbers.

Track 18

24											

Task 24

Write down the days of the month your hear.

Track 19

Task 25

More numbers. Listen and practise.

Track 20

erste	-	first	elfte	-	eleventh
zweite	-	second	zwölfte	-	twelfth
dritte	-	third	dreizehnte	-	thirteenth
vierte	-	fourth	vierzehnte	-	fourteenth
fünfte	-	fifth	fünfzehnte	-	fifteenth
sechste	-	sixth	sechzehnte	-	sixteenth
siebte	-	seventh	siebzehnte	-	seventeenth
achte	-	eighth	achtzehnte	-	eighteenth
neunte	-	ninth	neunzehnte	-	nineteenth
zehnte	-	tenth	zwanzigste	-	twentieth

Die Regel zur Bildung von Ordnungszahlen im Englischen ist, dass man an die Grundzahlen die Buchstaben **-th** hinzufügt. Ausgenommen sind**: first, second** und **third**.
Lernen Sie die Ordnungszahlen auswendig - das ist einfacher als die Regeln zu lernen. Bei zwanzig verändert sich die englische Endung **-y** von **twenty** in **-ieth**: **twentieth**. Dies gilt auch für dreißigste, vierzigste usw..

Im Deutschen gibt es Ordnungszahlen, die mit **eins, zwei, drei** beginnen, z. B. **einunddreißigste, zweiunddreißigste** oder **dreiunddreißigste**. Hierfür gilt im Englischen, dass die Begriffe **first, second** oder **third** nach den Zehnerzahlen gesetzt werden:

Es befindet sich auf der einundzwanzigsten Etage.
It is on the **twenty-first** floor.

Er wohnt in der zweiundvierzigsten Straße in New York.
He lives on **forty-second** Street in New York.

Dies ist die dreiunddreißigste Beschwerde.
This is the **thirty-third** complaint.

Beachten Sie, dass alle Zahlen über zwanzig durch einen Bindestrich verbunden werden:

twenty-one	twenty-first
thirty-three	thirty-third.

mostly	meistens
abbreviation	Abkürzung

In written language the English use abbreviations for first, second, third, fourth and so on.

This is mostly written as 1st, 2nd, 3rd, 4th, 14th, 21st, 32nd, 43rd, 55th, etcetera.

Task 26

Track 21

Listen to and repeat:

a hundred	a hundredth	100th
two hundred and sixty	two hundred and sixtieth	260th
a million	a millionth	
a billion	a billionth	

Den Zahlen werden ein 'a' oder 'one', 'two' usw. vorangestellt.

hundred	e.g. one hundred
thousand	one thousand
million	a million
billion	a billion

Task 27

Now make this exercise and pronounce and write the numbers out in full.
The first one is the example:

48th	62nd	91st	50th	100th
forty-eighth				
101st	102nd	103rd	104th	109th

Abbreviate the numbers in the right way.
The first one is the example:

thirty-second	fifteenth	twelfth	eleventh	twenty-first
32nd				
ninety-ninth	sixty-third	third	seventy-sixth	eighty-seventh

Task 28

Work in pairs. Speak and write. Take turns.

1. sechsunddreißigste ....
2. achtundvierzigste ....
3. siebenundachtzigste ....
4. fünfundsechzigste ....
5. vierundneunzigste ....
6. dreiundfünfzigste ....
7. zweiundsechzigste ....
8. neunundzwanzigste ....
9. dreiunddreißigste ....
10. einundneunzigste ....

Wenn im Deutschen ein Punkt steht, steht im Englischen ein Komma und umge-
kehrt

e. g.	Deutsch	Englisch
	2.714 km	2,714 km
	Euro 10,60	Euro 10.60
	19,8%	19.8%

Remember how to say:

703	seven hundred and three
521	five hundred and twenty-one
3,845	three thousand, eight hundred and forty-five
tel: 0904 - 37769	oh-nine-oh-four, three-double seven-six-nine
room 104	room one-oh-four / room one hundred and four
* 30 January 1988	the thirtieth of January nineteen eighty-eight

* Man kann auch schreiben:
    January 30,1988
    30th January 1988
    January 30th, 1988

Task 29

Now how do you say it?

1. Teilen Sie Ihrem Nachbarn mit, wie alt Sie sind.
2. Teilen Sie Ihrem Nachbarn mit, wie viele Geschwister Sie haben.
3. Teilen Sie Ihrem Nachbarn mit, wie viel Sie verdienen.
4. Sagen Sie, dass die Abteilung auf der siebten Etage ist.
5. Sagen Sie, dass Ihr Freund/ Ihre Freundin am neunten Geburtstag hat.

Task 30

Now listen to the spelling of some words. Put in a mark if it is correct.

Track 22

sam	kick	gem	jam	dog	cat	life	dress	grey

Task 31

People show up at the reception desk. They mention their names. They are asked
to spell them. Write down these names.

Track 23

1. Mrs. Blazer
2. ....
3. ....
4. ....
5. ....
6. ....

27

Task 32

What to say when?

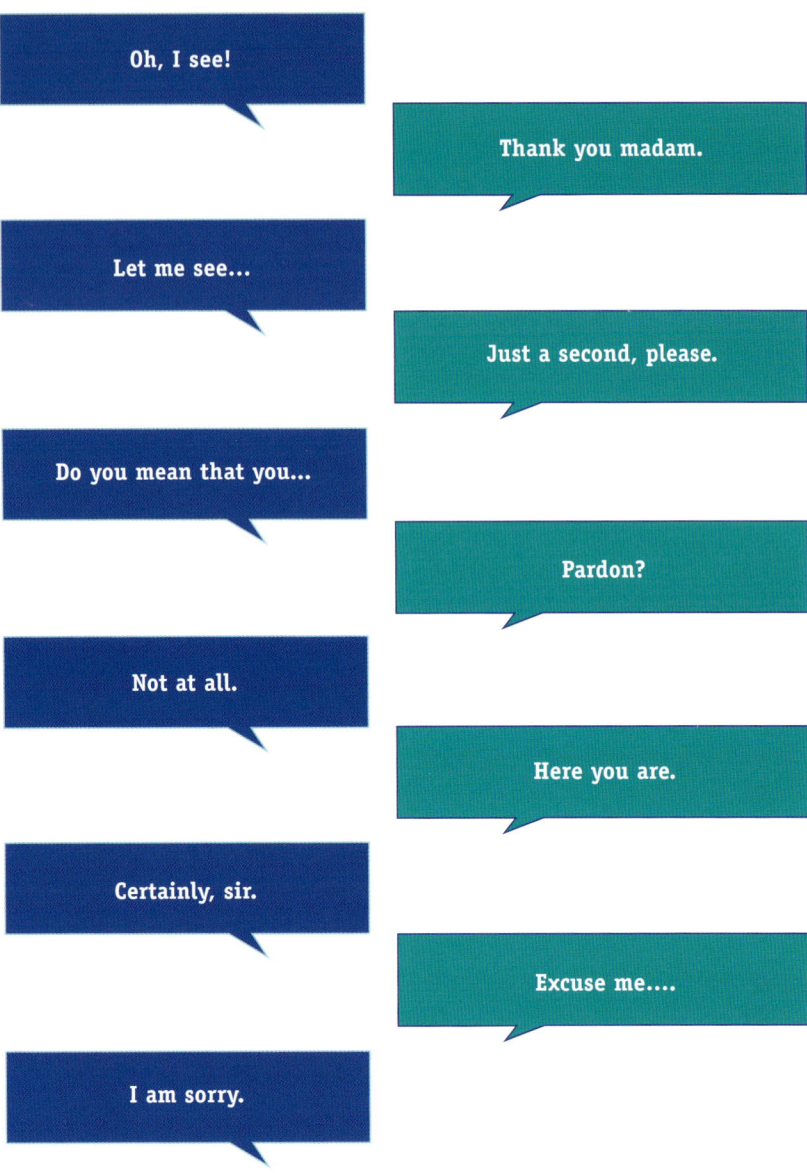

Use the expressions mentioned above. Write them down.

client	Kunde
torch	Taschenlampe
contract	Vertrag
colleague	Kollegin / Kollege

1. Sie reichen dem Besucher etwas an. ....
2. Sie bitten den Besucher zu verdeutlichen, was er meint. ....
3. Sie bitten um die Aufmerksamkeit des Kunden. ....
4. Sie reagieren auf das Dankeschön des Kunden. ....
5. Sie entschuldigen sich. ....
6. Sie bitten um ein wenig Geduld. ....
7. Sie möchten über ihr weiteres Vorgehen kurz nachdenken. ....
8. Sie geben dem Kunden zu erkennen, dass Sie ihm helfen können. ....
9. Sie machen deutlich, dass Sie den Kunden nicht verstehen. ....
10. Sie danken dem Besucher. ....
11. Sie lassen erkennen, dass Sie verstehen. ....

28

Sie müssen als Schutz- und Sicherheitskraft viele Fragen beantworten und auch selbst Fragen stellen. Sie haben es nun ein paar Mal geübt, aber es ist natürlich wichtig, zu wissen, wie man Fragen in Englisch stellt. Darum hier einige Regeln:

Wenn Sie in einem Satz eines der folgenden Wörter gebrauchen, ist die Bildung einer Frage ziemlich leicht, weil es ähnlich dem Deutschen ist**: can, may, might, shall, should, will, would, must, ought to, could, am, is, are, was, were.**
Stellen Sie eines dieser fettgedruckten Wörter an den Satzanfang und Sie haben eine Frage gebildet.
Es sind ziemlich viele Wörter, aber wenn Sie üben, geht es fast wie von selbst.

Beispiele:
Can I help you?   Kann ich Ihnen helfen?
Is that your torch?   Ist das deine Taschenlampe?

Wenn in einem Satz **have, has, had + Partizip Perfekt** gebraucht wird, dann wird **have, has** oder **had** an den Beginn des Satzes gestellt und schon haben Sie eine Frage gebildet.

Beispiele:
Have you had breakfast yet?   Hast du schon gefrühstückt?
Have you got my pen?   Hast du meinen Stift?

In allen anderen Fällen ist die Bildung einer Frage anders als im Deutschen. Im Englischen wird dafür **do, does** oder **did** gebraucht.
Do und **does** in der Gegenwart und **did** in der Vergangenheit.
Does gebraucht man bei he, she und it.
In anderen Fällen gebraucht man **do.**

Beispiele:
Do you live in Berlin?   Wohnst du in Berlin?
Does she have a contract?   Hat sie einen Vertrag?
Did Peter talk to his colleague?   Hat Peter mit seinem Kollegen gesprochen?

Task 33

Versuchen Sie, aus folgenden Sätzen Fragen zu bilden, wie im Beispiel.

| thief | Dieb |
| supervisor | Leiter, Aufseher |

1. The office is in the corner.
2. You can go that way.
3. Every visitor needs a badge to enter the building.
4. The thief went to the back of the house.
5. She shall see you to the door.
6. We need all the help we can get.
7. The supervisor talked to his men.
8. I would like to have a cup of coffee.
9. We'd like to see Mr. Turner.
10. You can pay over there.

1. Is the office in the corner?
2.
3.
4.
5.
6.
7.
8.
9.
10.

At the gate and behind the counter - meeting and greeting people

Mit den Grundlagen der englischen Sprache aus dem voran-
gegangenen Kapitel soll nun der Umgang mit Personen in
der Fremdsprache vertieft werden. Der Schwerpunkt wird auf
Situationen aus dem Pfortendienst gelegt und es wird aufgezeigt, wie man

* *ein Gespräch beginnt und abschließt*
* *einen Besucher empfängt oder warten lässt*
* *einem Besucher etwas anbietet*
* *Besuchern einfache Fragen stellt*
* *auf Fragen reagiert.*

Event

Thorsten and Corinna are safety and security specialists.
The two colleagues are on duty. They feel responsible for their jobs. People need
information. They expect them to have the right answers. So it is important to
the officers to find the right words and expressions. Indeed, people should feel
comfortable.
Depending on where you work sometimes there are visitors from abroad who have
many questions. Usually they will address you in English. So it's very important
that you can take part in these conversations and that you understand what
they're saying and be able to respond.

visitors	Besucher
security officer	Schutz- und Sicherheitskraft
colleague	Kollege
to be on duty	im Dienst sein
responsible	verantwortlich
job	Arbeit, Stelle
from abroad	aus dem Ausland

Task 1

Listen to the conversation.

Track 24

> Er...Good-morning.

> Can I help you?

> I am Thoma Watson from Los Angeles (handing her card).

would like to	würde gerne
of course	natürlich
to wait	warten

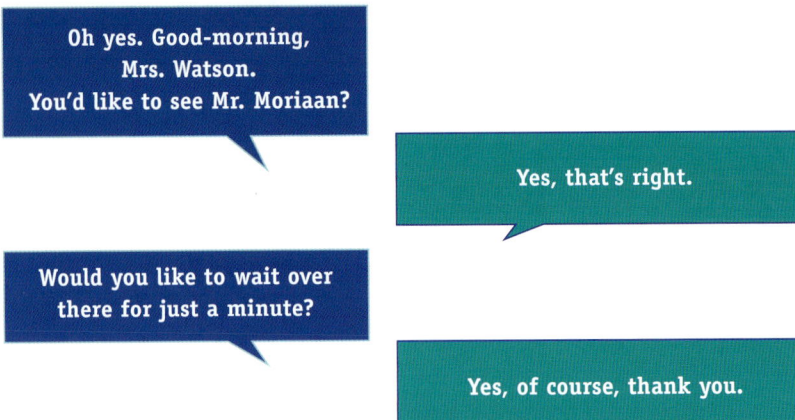

Oh yes. Good-morning, Mrs. Watson. You'd like to see Mr. Moriaan?

Yes, that's right.

Would you like to wait over there for just a minute?

Yes, of course, thank you.

Thoma Watson

district engineer

4354 Lennox Boulevard
Lennox, California 90304
678-3180
671-7153

Task 2

Go on listening and mark the expressions which are used.

Track 25   Your visitor has to wait:

Mrs. Watson, would you like:	
a cup of tea?	+ Yes, please
a cup of coffee?	+ Thank you
something to drink?	- No, thank you
to see the museum?	- No, that's all right.

Listen again and mark the appropriate expressions.

That's embarrassing!!	
I'm sorry, I hear Mr. Moriaan left.....ago	a minute five minutes half an hour an hour
I'm sure he'll be back...	later this afternoon soon in an hour in a minute at 3 o'clock

32

Would you...	like to wait? like to leave a message? like another drink?

Ah, there he is. Mr. Moriaan, this is Mrs. Watson from America.

Pleased to meet you.

Pleased to meet you, too.
I am so sorry I am late....

Task 3

Repeat listening to the conversation as a whole. Check if you marked the right answers. Practise with a partner. Take turns.

Track 26

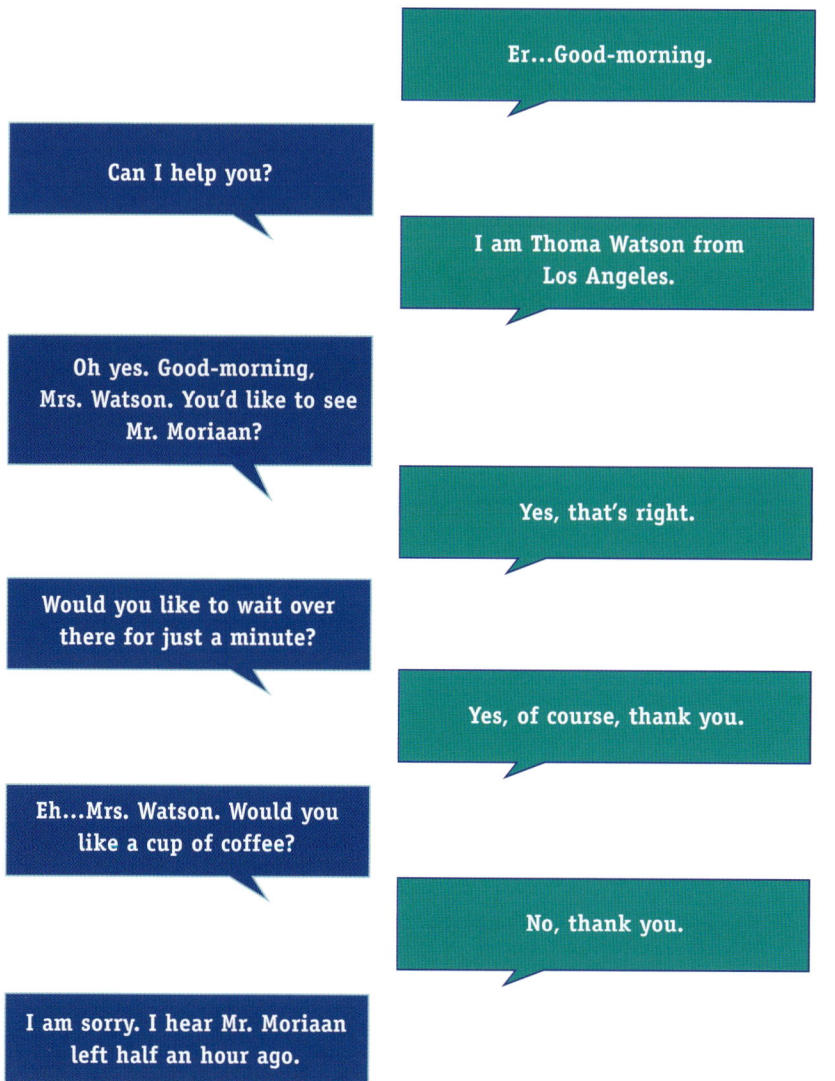

Er...Good-morning.

Can I help you?

I am Thoma Watson from Los Angeles.

Oh yes. Good-morning, Mrs. Watson. You'd like to see Mr. Moriaan?

Yes, that's right.

Would you like to wait over there for just a minute?

Yes, of course, thank you.

Eh...Mrs. Watson. Would you like a cup of coffee?

No, thank you.

I am sorry. I hear Mr. Moriaan left half an hour ago.

to repeat	wiederholen
as a whole	vollständig
madam	gnädige Frau
will	wird

33

When will he be back?

I am sure he'll be back in a minute. But would you like to leave a message perhaps?

No, that's all right.

Ah, there he is. Mr. Moriaan, this is Mrs. Watson from America.

Pleased to meet you.

Pleased to meet you, too. I am so sorry.

Task 4

Track 26

Listen to the dialogues of task 3 again. Work in pairs. Now match questions and answers yourselves. Switch roles.

Example: Möchten Sie...das Museum besuchen?
Start each question with.....'Would you like'......

Would you like to see the museum?

Ah, thank you.

1. Das Museum besuchen?
2. Einen Kaffee trinken?
3. Dort eben Platz nehmen?
4. Eine Nachricht hinterlassen?
5. Etwas trinken (have a soft drink?)
6. Eben warten?
7. Etwas essen (have a snack)?
8. Noch etwas trinken?

Possible answers:		
	Yes, please.	Gerne.
	No, thank you.	Nein, danke.
	Thank you.	Danke. Gerne.
	No, I'm alright.	Nein, danke.

34

Task 5

Study. How to say...

Guten Morgen.	Good morning.
Guten Tag. (Nachmittags)	Good afternoon.
Guten Abend.	Good evening.
Ich heiße..	My name is....
Ich bin...	I am...
Schön, Sie kennen zu lernen.	Pleased to meet you./ Nice to meet you.
Ich bin erfreut, Sie kennen zu lernen.	I'm delighted to meet you./ Nice to meet you.
Wie geht es Ihnen?	How are you?
Ich möchte Sie gerne.....vorstellen.	I'd like to introduce you to...
Dies ist...	This is...
Ich habe eine Verabredung mit...	I have an appointment with...
Ich werde ihn rufen.	I will call him.
Einen Moment bitte.	Just a moment, please.

Track 27

Task 6

Stellen Sie sich in Englisch vor.

A: Guten Morgen. Mein Name ist...
B: Guten Morgen. Nett, Sie kennen zu lernen. Ich heiße...
A: Schön, Sie kennen zu lernen.

Task 7

Stellen Sie sich gegenseitig in Englisch vor.

A: Begrüßt, nennt seinen Namen.
B: Grüßt zurück, nennt seinen Namen, stellt C vor.
A: Begrüßt C.
C: Grüßt A.

Task 8

Stellen Sie sich gegenseitig in Englisch vor.

A: Begrüßt, nennt seinen Namen.
B: Grüßt zurück, fragt, ob er helfen kann.
A: Sagt, dass er eine Verabredung mit C hat.
B: Sagt, dass er C rufen wird.

to disappoint	enttäuschen
to happen	passieren, ereignen
a. m.	vormittags
to look like	aussehen wie
male	männlich
tall	groß
service	Service, Dienst
to examine	untersuchen
case	Fall
glad	froh
to deal	behandeln
to be spoken to	angesprochen werden

Task 9

Work in pairs.
A client is disappointed in the help of one of your colleagues. She expects you to understand and be more positive.
The conversation must give information on:

Safety and security specialist	Client
• Where it has happened	in the car park
• What day it was	today
• What time it was	9.30 a.m.
• What the colleague looks like	male/ tall/ blond hair
• What the name is	no idea
• The service will examine the case	glad to hear that
• These problems are dealt with care	I understand
• The colleague involved will be spoken to	thank you

Complete this dialogue. Practise it. Take turns.

Safety and security specialist   **Client**

1. Good morning officer. I am so disappointed.

2. Good morning, madam. I am sorry to hear that.

3. It's about your colleague. About his help.

4. What happened?

Etc.

Task 10

Study these boxes. Work in pairs. Match questions and answers. Take turns.

You like to...	You say...	You respond...
...sagen, dass jemand vor 5 Minuten weggegangen ist (eine halbe Stunde, zwei Stunden)	He left five minutes ago. (half an hour, two hours)	When will he be back?
...sagen, dass Sie sich sicher sind, dass er umgehend zurück sein wird (morgen, heute Mittag, um zwei Uhr)	I'm sure he'll be back in a minute (tomorrow, this afternoon, at two o'clock)	All right, I'll wait. I'll come back tomorrow then.

...fragen, ob jemand eine Nachricht hinterlassen möchte.	Would you like to leave a message?	Yes, please. No, thank you.
...jemanden begrüßen, ein Gespräch beginnen.	Good-morning (Good afternoon). Can I help you?	Yes, I would like to talk to...
...jemanden bitten, dort Platz zu nehmen.	Would you like to wait over there for just a minute?	Yes, of course, thank you.
...jemanden vorstellen.	This is Mr..., Mrs...., Miss...	Pleased to meet you. How do you do?
...jemanden begrüßen, den Sie zum ersten Mal treffen/ kennen lernen.	Pleased to meet you.	Pleased to meet you, too.

Example:

Good afternoon, can I help you?
Yes, I would like to talk to...

Task 11

Study the conversation. Work with a partner. Make a note (=keyword) in each box. Create your sentences. Practise your dialogue. Switch roles.

appointment	Verabredung
note	Anmerkung, Vermerk
keyword	Schlüsselwort
to create	bilden

My name is Miss Jones and I have an appointment with Mrs. Waldmann.

Sagen Sie, dass es Ihnen leid tut, aber sie vor einer halben Stunde weggegangen ist.

When will she be back?

Geben Sie zu verstehen, dass Sie nicht verstanden haben.

When will she be back?

Sagen Sie, dass Sie sicher sind, dass sie umgehend zurückkommt.

Well, I hope so.

Fragen Sie, ob sie warten will oder eine Nachricht hinterlassen möchte.

No,...

Bieten Sie ihr einen Kaffee oder Tee an.

Yes, please. I'd like a cup of coffee.

Task 12

Work out this dialogue as you did in task 11.

Begrüßen Sie die Person und beginnen Sie das Gespräch.

My name is Mrs. Wood.

Erinnern Sie sich. Sollte die Verabredung mit Frau Pfeiffer um zwei Uhr stattfinden?

Yes, that's right.

Bitten Sie sie, kurz Platz zu nehmen, da Frau Pfeiffer gerade eben weggegangen ist.

Oh, I see. When will she be back?

Sagen Sie, dass sie vor 1 Stunde gegangen ist, aber in einer halben Stunde wieder zurück sein wird.

I'm very sorry, but I cannot wait that long.

Fragen Sie, ob sie eine Nachricht hinterlassen möchte.

No, thank you. Just tell her I'll be back tomorrow.

Erklären Sie Ihr Einverständnis und sagen Sie nochmals, dass es Ihnen Leid tut. Verabschieden Sie sich mit 'See you tomorrow.'

All right. Bye-bye.

05

At the gate and on patrol - giving directions

Als Schutz- und Sicherheitskraft werden Sie in verschiedenen Aufgabenbereichen - ob bei Empfangsdiensten im Rahmen eines Telefonates, bei Einsätzen auf einem Gelände oder im öffentlichen Raum, z. B. bei Veranstaltungen - oftmals nach dem Weg gefragt. Im Folgenden werden Ihnen Beispiele aufgezeigt, wie Sie in englischer Sprache einen Weg oder eine Anreise, auch mit Hilfe von Zeichnungen oder Plänen, beschreiben können. Sie erfahren zudem, wie Sie sich vorstellen und wie Sie Namen von Kunden bzw. Gästen erfragen können.

Task 1

You are a security staff member or a guard. You are on surveillance on the premises. Knowing your way about is essential for helping people out. Words and expressions come in handy then. Listen and practise. Learn them by heart.

Track 28

1. left	a. links	to know	wissen
2. turn left	b. biegen Sie / biege links ab	expression	Ausdruck
3. right	c. rechts	to come in handy	gut gebrauchen können
4. traffic lights	d. Verkehrsampel	to learn by heart	auswendig lernen
5. go straight ahead	e. gehe/ gehen Sie geradeaus	guard	Wachposten
6. take the 1st street on the left	f. nimm/ nehmen Sie die erste Straße links		
7. walk down the street	g. laufe/ laufen Sie die Straße weiter runter		
8. it is opposite	h. es ist gegenüber		
9. it is next to	i. es ist neben		
10. it is near here	j. es ist hier in der Nähe		
11. in front of you	k. vor dir /vor Ihnen		
12. go through the shop	l. gehe/ gehen Sie durch das Geschäft		
13. take the stairs to	m. nehmen Sie die Treppe zur / zum		
14. take the lift/ elevator	n. nehmen Sie den Aufzug		
15. take the escalator	o. nehmen Sie die Rolltreppe		
16. cross the street	p. überqueren Sie die Straße		
17. crossroads/ intersection(s)	q. Kreuzung(en)		
18. the entrance	r. der Eingang		
19. around the corner	s. um die Ecke		
20. you pass it	t. Du kommst/ Sie kommen daran vorbei.		

41

Task 2

Track 29

Listen to the conversation.

Customer: Excuse me, can you tell me where the tourist office is?
Assistant: Yes, of course. Leave the building through the main entrance.
             Turn left and at the crossroads turn right. Go straight ahead and
             you will see the tourist office in front of you.
Customer: Thank you.
Assistant: Don't mention it.

tourist office	Touristikzentrale
to leave	verlassen
crossroads	Kreuzung
straight ahead	geradeaus

Task 3

Track 30

Listen to the conversation.

Customer: Excuse me, where are the toilets?
Assistant: They are in the restaurant, which is on the top floor.
Customer: Is it accessible for wheelchairs?
Assistant: Oh, there's a special toilet here on the ground floor. It's behind
             the stairs. Go straight ahead, pass the cash desks and then it's on
             your left.
Customer: Thank you.

access	Zugang
wheelchair	Rollstuhl
stairs	Treppe

Task 4

Study the ground-plan of this company. There are three floors: the basement, the ground floor and the first floor. On the ground floor you find the reception and rooms G1 to G6. On the first floor you find rooms 101 to 107. In the basement you find various departments. They are all connected by corridors and lifts*.

*Im amerikanischen Englisch bezeichnet man Fahrstühle meistens mit 'elevator'.

company	Firma
floor	Etage, Stockwerk
basement	Untergeschoss
ground floor	Parterre
various	verschiedene
department	Abteilung
to connect	verbinden
corridor	Gang
elevator	Aufzug
gents	Herrentoilette
post room	Poststelle
storeroom	Magazin
switchboard	Empfang/ Zentrale
to have	haben
to have to	müssen

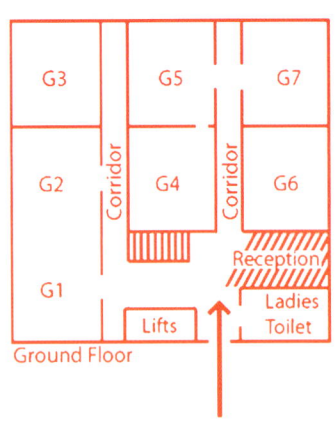

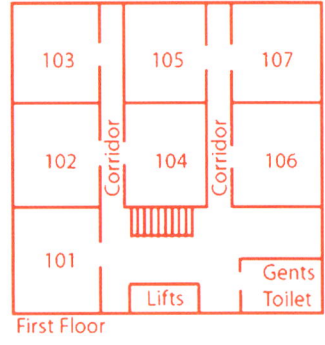

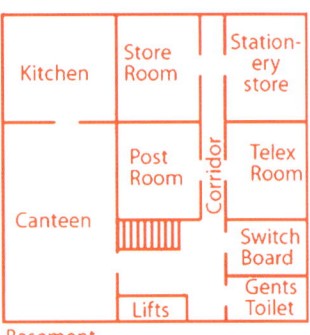

Corinna as a safety and security specialist is giving information to clients who are looking for certain destinations. Listen to the information. Find the places where clients have to go. Use the ground-plan of the company. Please fill in the blanks.

Track 31

| Client | 1. | Excuse me, where is the Gents? |
| Corinna | | Take the lift or the stairs to the first floor. The Gents' is next to the lift in the corner. |

| Client | 2. | Excuse me, where can I find the library? |
| Corinna | | That's on the first floor. Take the corridor on your left. It's the first room on your right, room 104. |

| Client | 3. | Excuse me, could you tell me where the canteen is, please? |
| Corinna | | Yes, of course. You will find the canteen in the basement. When you step out of the lift it's on your left-hand side. |

Client	4.	Wants to go...
Client	5.	Wants to go...
Client	6.	Wants to go...

Im Bezug auf Etagen gibt es Unterschiede zwischen dem amerikanischen und britischen Englisch. Beide gebrauchen das Wort 'floor' und die Amerikaner außerdem das Wort 'storey'. Es gibt auch noch Unterschiede in Bezug auf die Höhe der Stockwerke:

GB	US	D
ground floor first floor second floor etc.	first floor or first storey second storey third storey	Erdgeschoss erste Etage zweite Etage

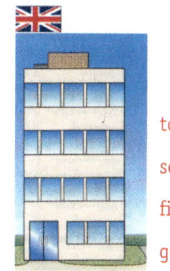

fourth floor
third floor
second floor
first floor

top floor
second floor
first floor
ground floor

Task 5

Work in pairs. Work out three dialogues. Show people the way. Still use the ground-plan of the company. Take turns. Use this information:

a. The client has an appointment with Mr. Fischer. Mr. Fischer is on the first floor in room 105.
b. The client likes to see Mrs. Schneider. She is in the post room.
c. The client has to go to Mrs. Weinberger. Normally she is in room G1. But not today. Now she is in G2.

Task 6

Again use the ground-plan of the company. Fill in the blanks.

1. Which room is opposite the stationery store? ....
2. Which room is between G1 and G3? ....
3. Which room is next to the telex room? ....
4. What's in front of the switch-board? ....
5. What is near the reception? ....
6. Which room is between the stationary store and the switch-board? ....
7. Which room is opposite G5? ....

8. When you come out of the lift
   on the first floor you take the
   corridor on the right. It's on the left.   ....

9. When you come out of the lift
   in the basement, it's on the left   ....

10. When you come into the
    building on the ground floor,
    take the corridor on the right.
    It's on the left.   ....

11. When you come out of the lift
    in the basement, take the
    corridor on the right. It's on the
    right.   ....

12. Take the stairs to the first floor.
    It's on your left next to the lift.   ....

Task 7

Note!

to note	zur Kenntnis nehmen
direction	Richtung
town	Stadt
to reach	erreichen
main road	Hauptstraße
church road	Kirchstraße
spot	Platz
platform	Bahnsteig
to get downtown	in die (Innen-)Stadt kommen
to make notes	Notizen machen

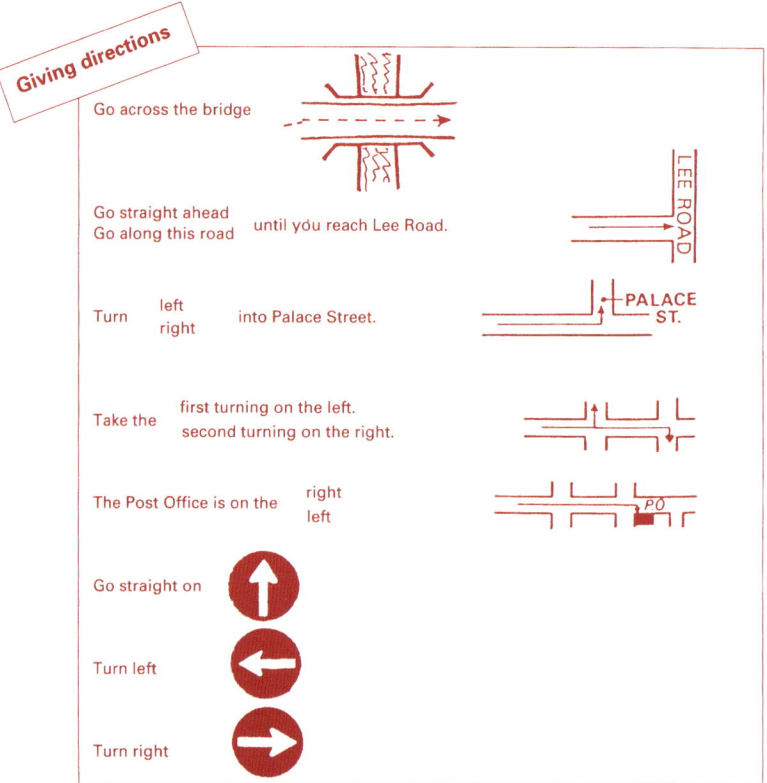

Study the map. You are at the station. Listen to the 3 dialogues. Listen to the directions that are told. Put the letters A, B, and C in the right spots on the map. Check your answers by listening again.

Track 32

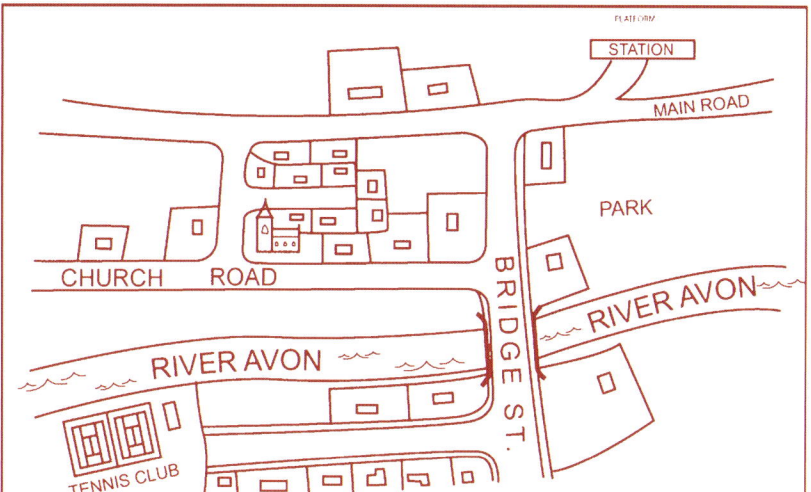

Task 8

Track 33

How to get downtown? Listen to the telephone conversation. Use the boxes to put your answers in.

- Make notes in boxes 1, 2 and 3 to tell in what places to find the bus, the subway and a taxi.
- Make notes in boxes 4, 5 and 6 if it is a problem to do so.
- Tick one of the smaller boxes to tell how to get downtown.

terrific	großartig
suddenly	plötzlich
to have two weeks off	zwei Wochen frei haben
invitation	Einladung
to stay	bleiben
subway	U-Bahn

	Where is it?	What problem?
The bus?	1	4
The subway?	2	5
A taxi?	3	6

Task 9

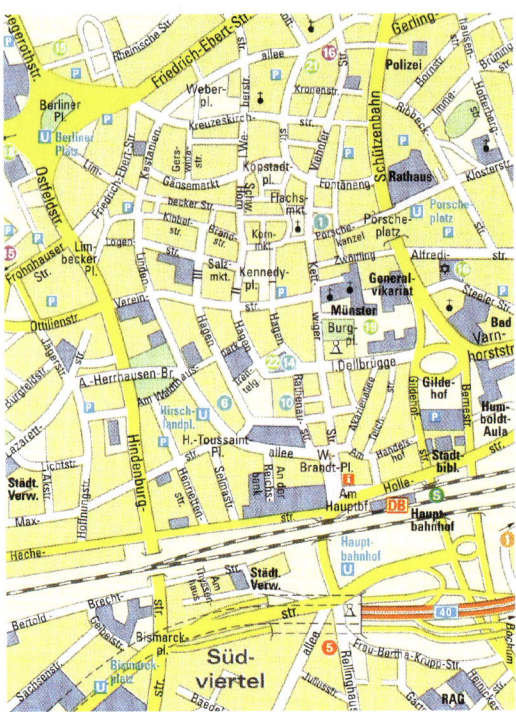

Track 34

Have a close look at the map of the town. Listen to and copy the example.
Switch roles.

> **Excuse me. Could you tell me where the main station is?**

> **Certainly. You are now at the Hindenburgstraße. Take the second street left. That's Hachestraße. The main station is past the post office on your right.**

> **Thanks a lot.**

> **Not at all. Good-bye.**

main station	Hauptbahnhof
T-crossing	T-Kreuzung
main entrance	Haupteingang
synagogue	Synagoge

Do it again, but now listen to the question of your partner and have a look at the map. You are at the main entrance at Hollestraße at the main station.
Use words "to buy some time", like:
"Let me see..",
"Just a minute, please...",
"Well...erm...where is...",
"Oh yes, ..".

Where to go to?

Questions A
1　Hirschlandplatz?
2　Porscheplatz?
3　Synagogue?

Questions B
1　Lindenallee?
2　Limbecker Platz?
3　Bismarckplatz?

46

Task 10

Match the English and German words. The first one has already been done for you.

A. go straight ahead		1. Platz	
B. traffic lights		2. Richtung	
C. crossroads		3. Sackgasse	
D. traffic signs		4. geradeaus gehen	
E. a roundabout		5. Weg, Pfad	
F. direction		6. Ampelanlage	
G. bend		7. Kreuzung	
H. alley		8. Kurve	
I. square		9. Verkehrsschilder	
J. circus		10. Kreisverkehr	
K. dead-end-street		11. (runder) Platz	

A	B	C	D	E	F	G	H	I	J	K
4										

Task 11

Christine is on duty on the reception desk of the Silbermüller AG in Essen (TOR 1). Opposite of it is the car park. She attends to the carpark. Listen to the conversation. Work in pairs. Switch roles.

Track 35

47

opposite	gegenüber
car park	Parkplatz
barrier	Schlagbaum
to attend to	sorgen für
road constructions	Straßenbauarbeiten
ground plan / a map	Geländeplan
entrance	Eingang
to check	kontrollieren
production	Produktion
canteen	Kantine
plant maintenance	Wartungsabteilung
workshop	Werkstatt
disposal	Abfallentsorgung
dispatch	Versand

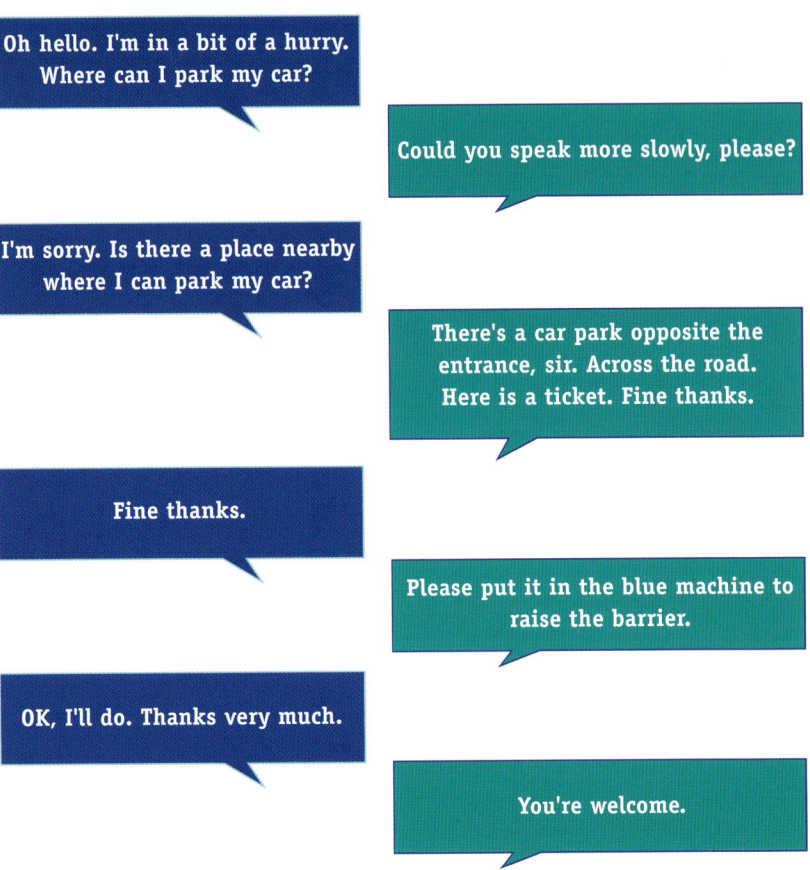

Task 12

Use the ground plan of the premises. Write down some questions.

Where is the car park?	It's across the road.
.............................?	It's behind the parking at TOR 5.
.............................?	It's between the laboratory store and TOR 3.
.............................?	It's opposite the polyethers-works 4.
.............................?	It's near the truck-scale 2.
.............................?	It's in front of the OS-works.
.............................?	It's next to the Silbermüller AG.

Task 13

spot	Platz
administration	Verwaltung
fire department	Feuerwehr
research department	Forschungsabteilung
police department	Polizei
computer centre	Rechenzentrum
sales department	Verkaufsabteilung
central station	Hauptbahnhof

Look at the map. Now you tell the way. Work in pairs. Take turns. Always start at the spot marked with a cross.

1. Excuse me, could you tell me how I can get to the administration (1)?
2. Excuse me, how do I reach the fire department (2)?
3. Excuse me, where can we find a cafeteria (3)?
4. Excuse me, where is the police department (4)?
5. Excuse me, we are looking for the computer centre (5)?
6. Excuse me, is there a hospital (6) nearby?
7. Excuse me, sales department (7). How do I get there?
8. Excuse me, where can we find a bank (8)?

48

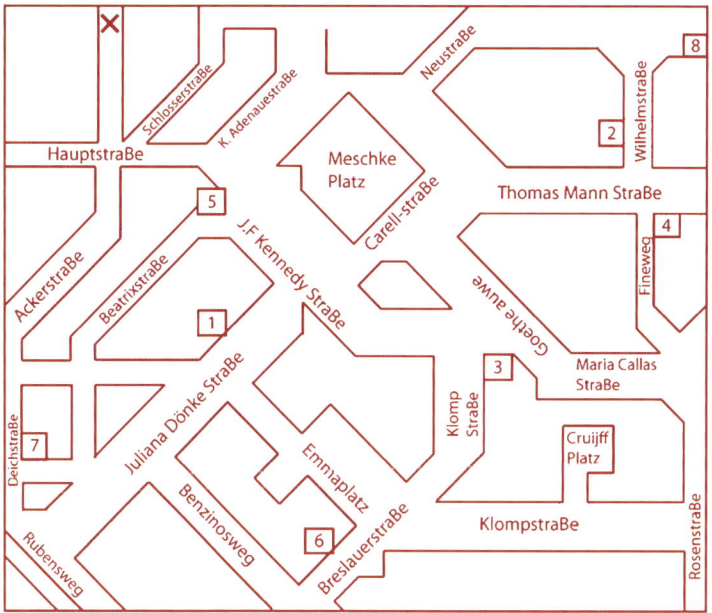

Task 14

Look at the next map. You are on surveillance. You are at the local bus station in the hall where the information centre is. People ask for your help. Listen and show them the way. Use the abbreviations and put them in the right place on the map.

Track 36

abbreviation	Abkürzung
to mention	erwähnen
hairdresser's	Friseursalon
chemist's	Drogerie

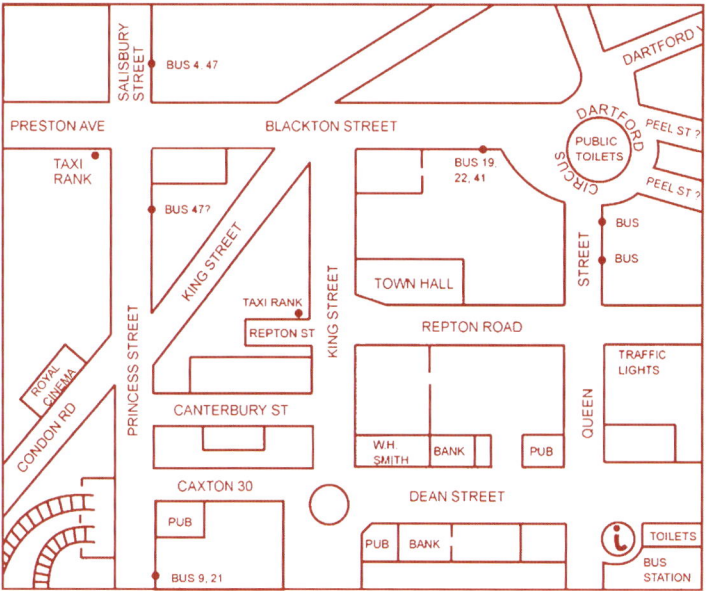

the post office	P.O.
a restaurant	Rest.
number 32 busstop	Bus.
the railway station	Rail.
a chemist's	Chem.
a hairdresser's	Hairdr.

Task 15

Note!
How to ask to go where? Study the ways of saying. Keep them in mind.

to keep in mind	nicht vergessen
to sound	klingen
complicated	schwierig
short	kurz
to stand for	bedeuten

49

How do I get to...?
Can you tell me the way to...?
Can/ could you tell me where the...............is, please?

Now study the map of a town in Germany.

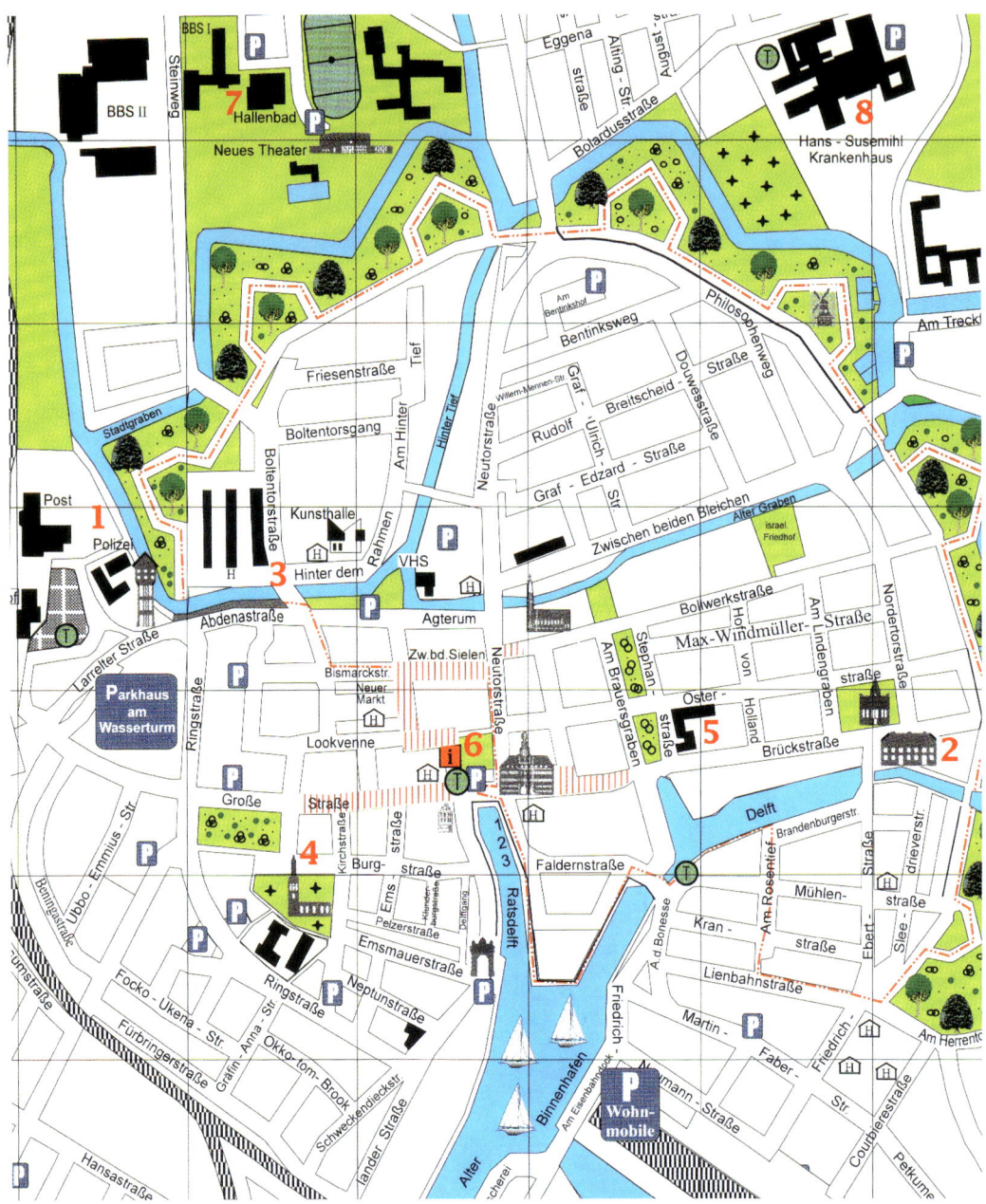

Figures 1 to 8 stand for:

1. police station   2. library
3. bus station   4. church
5. school   6. tourist information office
7. swimming pool   8. hospital

Work with a partner. Look at the dialogues. Prepare on paper first and then play the roles.

A   Start   at the bus station
    Arrival   at the hospital
    Question   Excuse me, could you tell me where the hospital is?
    Route   Certainly,...

50

B   Start   at school
    Arrival   at the library
    Question   Can you tell me how to get to the library?
    Route   Well,...

C   Start   at the library
    Arrival   at Neutorstraße
    Question   How do I get to Neutorstraße ?
    Route   ....

D   Start   at the church
    Arrival   at the police station
    Question   Where...?
    Route   ....

E   Start   in the Bolardusstraße
    Arrival   at the swimming pool
    Question   ...the shortest way to...?
    Route   ....

Task 16

Work in pairs. Again study the map. Find out where to go (=arrival). You know where to start. You show how to find it (=route).

Example:
Start   at the police station
Route   Turn left into Abdenastraße. Go along this street till you come to the crossroads. Turn left into Boltentorstraße. Go straight ahead till you cross the canal and come to Steinweg.
Arrival   On the left hand side you see.........

Now work out 6 more examples to find out where the arrivals are. Prepare on paper first, then play them. Take turns.

Task 17

Study the ground-plan. Listen to the dialogue. Use it as an example.

Track 37

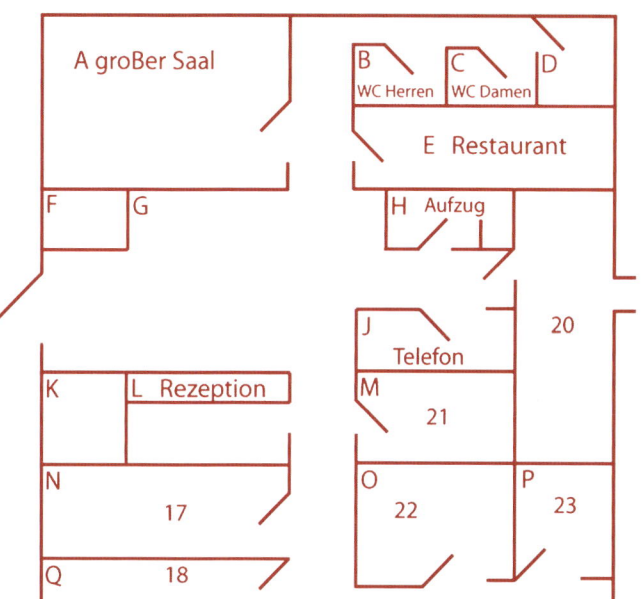

51

> **Guten Morgen.**

> **Good morning. Could you tell me where room 23 is?**

> **Certainly, madam. Walk down this passage. Turn left at the end. Room 23 is the second room on your left.**

> **Thank you.**

> **Not at all.**

You are at the reception desk. Clients need information. They ask for:

1. the gent's toilets
2. the bar
3. room 18
4. room 117....on the first floor, opposite the lift.

Work in pairs. Work out 4 dialogues. Prepare on paper. Then check your answers with the conversations. Play them and switch roles.

Task 18

You are on surveillance in town.
People have more questions:

1. Where is the shopping-centre?
2. Is there a restaurant nearby?
3. Is the post office nearby?

Work with a partner. Use a map of your town. You start at your college. Find the routes. Work out 3 dialogues. Prepare on paper. Then play the roles and take turns.

06//

At the reception desk - telephoning

Wie im privaten Leben spielt auch in nahezu allen Funktionen der Schutz- und Sicherheitskraft das Telefon eine große Rolle. In diesem Kapitel wird der Schwerpunkt auf das Telefonieren in der englischen Sprache mit Kunden und/oder Auftraggebern gelegt. Ihnen werden mögliche Formulierungen für das Annehmen, Weiterleiten und Beenden von Telefonaten vermittelt und wie Sie Nachrichten aufnehmen können.

Event

A security team is on duty at the reception desk. Clients are on the phone, having all kinds of questions. You have to carry out correctly various activities (at the same time):

knowing how to respond
knowing how to:
- put people through
- put messages through
- fill in forms

Task 1

In speaking on the telephone there are ways of saying which are of great help to you. Study and memorize them.

Wenn Sie eine Person sprechen möchten oder mit einer bestimmten Abteilung verbunden werden möchten, sagen Sie:

- Can I talk to Mr. Wainwright, please?
- I'd like to speak to Mr. Wainwright, please.
- Can you put me through to the manager, please?
- I'd like to speak to the manager, please.
- Can you put me through to the research department?

Wenn ein Anrufer am Apparat bleiben bzw. warten soll, sagen Sie:
- One moment, please.
- Hold on, please.
- Hold the line, please.

way of saying	Ausdrucksweise
to memorize	auswendig lernen
manager	Manager, Betriebsleiter
toy	Spielzeug
extension	Nebenanschluss, Apparat
engaged	besetzt
to try	versuchen

Wenn Sie einen Anrufer verbinden, sagen Sie:
- I'll put you through.

Wenn die Leitung besetzt oder die betreffende Person, zu der durchgestellt werden soll, im Gespräch ist, sagen Sie:
- I'm sorry, the extension is engaged.
- I'm sorry. He/she is on another line.
- Im sorry. The line is busy.

Wenn Sie um einen Rückruf bitten möchten, sagen Sie:
- Could you ask him/her if he/she can call me back, please?
- Could you ask him/her to call me back, please?

Wenn Sie jemanden bitten müssen, später zurückzurufen, sagen Sie:
- Could you call back tomorrow?
- Can you try again later?

Wenn Sie die Nummer des Anrufers wissen möchten, sagen Sie:
- Can I have your number, please?

Wenn Sie wissen möchten, ob Sie eine Nachricht entgegen nehmen sollen, sagen Sie:
- Can I give him/ her a message?
- Can I take a message?

Wenn Sie den Namen des Anrufers brauchen, sagen Sie:
- Can I have your name, please?

Wenn der Anrufer seinen Namen buchstabieren soll, sagen Sie:
- Could you spell your name, please?

Task 2

How to say in German?

1. Can I talk to Mr. Wainwright, please?
2. I'd like to speak to Mr. Wainwright, please.
3. Can you put me through to the research department?
4. One moment, please.
5. Hold the line, please.
6. I'll put you through.
7. I'm sorry, the extension is engaged.
8. Could you ask him/her if he/she can call me back, please?
9. Could you call back tomorrow?
10. Can you try again later?
11. Can I have your number, please?
12. Could you please tell him/her that I've called and give him/her my message, please?
13. Can I take a message?
14. Can I have your name and number, please?
15. Could you spell your name, please?

Task 3

Complete the telephone conversation in English.

manager	Abteilungsleiter
extension	Durchwahl

Receptionist   Good morning. Anson's Security.
Caller   Fragen Sie, ob Sie den Abteilungsleiter sprechen könnten.
Receptionist   One moment, I'll see if he is in. I'm sorry, he isn't in today.
Caller   Fragen Sie, ob Sie eine Nachricht hinterlassen können.
Receptionist   That's possible.
Caller   Bitten Sie um einen Rückruf unter 0221 - 678995 mit der Durchwahl 15.

Task 4

Translate this telephone conversation into English.

to translate	übersetzen

Caller   Guten Morgen. Sie sprechen mit Frau Smith. Kann ich Herrn Grieves sprechen?
Telephonist   Einen Augenblick bitte, ich verbinde Sie weiter. Es tut mir leid, seine Leitung ist besetzt. Wollen Sie warten oder kann ich eine Nachricht weiterleiten?
Caller   Können Sie ihn bitten, mich zurückzurufen?
Telephonist   Natürlich. Können Sie bitte Ihren Namen buchstabieren?
Caller   S-M-I-T-H
Telephonist   Wie lautet Ihre Nummer, bitte?
Caller   0044 -351-268341.
Telephonist   Vielen Dank. Ich werde ihm die Nachricht weitergeben.

Task 5

Telephone numbers are pronounced in a different way. Listen and repeat them.

Track 38

5212497	local call

020-5644722 035-6462038	trunk call/long-distance call
0341-662297 0342-643369	

trunk call	Ferngespräch
distance	Entfernung
from abroad	aus dem Ausland

0031-55-2093644	international call/calling abroad
09-39-547-300457 0031-55-2923644	

Task 6

Write down the telephone numbers.

Track 39

764025				

Task 7

Track 40

Listen to the conversations. Fill in the blanks.

to call	anrufen
afternoon	Nachmittag
ticket office	Theaterkasse
to reserve seats	Plätze reservieren
of course	natürlich
to collect	abholen
wallet	Brieftasche
to require	benötigen
waiting list	Warteliste
advance	Fortschritt
single room	Einzelzimmer
available	erhältlich
cancellation	Absage

Conversation 1

Telephonist	Good............Jackson's..........can I................you?
Caller	Can I.....................to the manager,........................?
Telephonist	What's...?
Caller	......................me. My name is Mr. Ferguson.
Telephonist	..................the ....,please. I'll see if he is in.
Telephonist	Mr. Ferguson?
Caller	Yes?
Telephonist	..............you......................................in the afternoon, the manager is in a........................at the moment.
Caller	I'm afraid that's not ....,can I.......................... a..............................?
Telephonist	Of course!
Caller	Please,...........................him I can't.............to the manager's meeting................
Telephonist	I've .... a.............................of it.
Caller	Thank you,...........................
Telephonist	Good bye.

Conversation 2

Telephonist	Good...............Jackson's................can I ....you?
Caller	Can you.................me.................to the ticket office?
Telephonist	...........please. I'll......................you........................
Secretary	Good..................,ticket office..................... I ....you?
Caller	I...................like to reserve......................seats for the ....tonight.
Secretary	That's......................,what's...........................name, please?
Caller	My name is...............................
Secretary	Can you...........................that, ...?
Caller	Of course,...................is...
Secretary	........................you like seats at.................or .... pounds?
Caller	I'll.................the seats at...................pounds.
Secretary	You...............collect the tickets.............................one hour......................the concert starts.
Caller	I'll...........................Thank you very much.
Secretary	Alright Mr. Reed...................tickets....................be waiting for you. Goodbye.
Caller	Goodbye.

Conversation 3

Telephonist	Good.................. Jackson's..............can I ....you?
Caller	Good..............................., my..................is Mrs. Peach. This ....I was at your............ but I...................... I left my wallet at the......................... Could ....please............... me if a wallet was found?
Telephonist	One...................,please. I'll...............at the customer information desk.
Telephonist	Hello.............................?
Caller	Yes?

Telephonist	The......................found your wallet. You..............collect it at the customer information desk.
Caller	...................goodness, that you.................it. What time does the shop close?
Telephonist	The shop is open until seven........................
Caller	I see,...
Telephonist	You're......................,goodbye.
Caller	Goodbye.

Check the answers with the texts.

Task 8

Listen to the first caller and fill in the reservation form.

Track 41

Reservation form

Name of guest: Mr/Mrs/Miss/Ms..

Address:................................. Arrival date:.................................
....

How many nights:..............................

Telephone:...........................

single ☐   single bath ☐   single shower ☐

double ☐   double bath ☐   double shower ☐   twin bath ☐

Rate per night:............................... Clerk:...............................

How many people:......................... Date:...............................

---

quiet	ruhig
bill	Rechnung
market	Markt

Task 9

Listen to the second caller and fill in the reservation form.

Track 42

Reservation form

Name of guest: Mr/Mrs/Miss/Ms..

Address:................................. Arrival date:.................................
....

How many nights:..............................

Telephone:...........................

single ☐   single bath ☐   single shower ☐

double ☐   double bath ☐   double shower ☐   twin bath ☐

Rate per night:............................... Clerk:...............................

How many people:......................... Date:...............................

---

shower	Dusche
full board	Vollpension
daily	täglich
rate	Preis
space	Raum
confirmation	Bestätigung

Task 10

Listen to the third caller and fill in the reservation form.

operator	Telefonist (in)
twinbedded	mit zwei Betten
continental	europäisch, kontinental
breakfast	Frühstück
postal code	Postleitzahl
to look forward to	sich freuen auf
to prefer	bevorzugen

Reservation form

Name of guest: Mr/Mrs/Miss/Ms..

Address:.................................... Arrival date:..................................

....

How many nights:............................

Telephone:...............................

single ☐ single bath ☐ single shower ☐

double ☐ double bath ☐ double shower ☐ twin bath ☐

Rate per night:............................... Clerk:...............................

How many people:........................... Date:...............................

Task 11

Check your answers of tasks 8-10 with the texts.

First caller

Caller	Good morning. This is Frau Schmidt of Holstein AG, Hamburg. I want to reserve a single room for Herr Lang, our Marketing Manager.
Receptionist	Yes, Frau Schmidt. When does he require the room?
Caller	For the night of the 24th August. And Herr Lang would like a quiet room away from the street.
Receptionist	For the 24th August. Certainly. Could you give me your address, please?
Caller	Yes it's Postweg 45, 21075 Hamburg.
Receptionist	Could you spell 'Postweg', please?
Caller	Yes, it's P-O-S-T-W-E-G.
Receptionist	Postweg 45, 21075 Hamburg.
Caller	Right. Oh, and would you send us the bill, please?
Receptionist	Of course. And thank you for calling.
Caller	Thank you. Goodbye.

Second caller

Receptionist	Advance Reservations. Can I help you?
Caller	Yes, do you have a double room with shower from the 19th to the 23rd August, with full board, please?
Receptionist	One moment, please...Yes, we have.
Caller	What is the daily rate?
Receptionist	D.kr. 340 per person.
Caller	Fine. Could I make a booking, please?
Receptionist	Certainly. Your name, address and telephone number, please.

58

Caller	My name is Roberts and the address is P.O. Box 743, NL-1017 Amsterdam. The telephone is 02164572. Could I also have garage space for my car?
Receptionist	Certainly, Mr. Roberts. I'll reserve you a space. Anything else, sir?
Caller	No, that's all, thank you.
Receptionist	I'll send you a confirmation of your booking.
Caller	Thank you very much. Goodbye.
Receptionist	Goodbye.

Third caller

Operator	Hotel Regent. Good morning. Can I help you?
Caller	Yes, I'd like to book a room for next week.
Operator	Hold the line, please, and I'll put you through to Advance Reservations.
Receptionist	Advance Reservations. Can I help you?
Caller	Yes. I'd like to book a twinbedded room from the afternoon of the 21st August to the morning of the 27th.
Receptionist	Yes, we have a twinbedded room available for those dates. The rate is 70 per night, including continental breakfast.
Caller	That will be fine.
Receptionist	Could I have your name and address, please?
Caller	Yes, it's Mr. James.
Receptionist	J-A-M-E-S.
Caller	Yes, that's right. 42, Station Road, York, England.
Receptionist	Have you the post code, please?
Caller	Yes, it's YO2 1JG.
Receptionist	42, Station Road, York YO2 1JG, England...Good. And your telephone number?
Caller	090453666
Receptionist	Right. Thank you. I'll send you a reservation card by post confirming your booking, Mr. James. And we look forward to your visit.
Caller	Thank you very much. Goodbye.
Receptionist	Goodbye, sir.

Task 12

Use a dictionary if necessary. Fill in the blanks in the German language. Find the English expressions in the texts mentioned above. Underline them.

1. Hold the line.	1. ....
2. I'll put you through.	2. ....
3. A twinbedded room.	3. ....
4. A continental breakfast.	4. ....
5. We look forward to your visit.	5. ....
6. A cancellation.	6. ....
7. The bill.	7. ....
8. A double room with shower.	8. ....
9. Full board.	9. ....
10. The daily rate.	10. ....

answering machine	Anrufbeantworter
to represent	gegenwärtig sein
sophisticated	hoch entwickelt
issue	Angelegenheit
branch office	Filiale
fair	Messe
to exchange	austauschen

Task 13

You work for Best-Sec Guarding.

The address is
Best-Sec Guarding Essen
Markelplatz 17
42166 Essen
Telefon: 0201 - 3789310
Telefax: 0201 - 4437845

This morning there is a message on the telephone answering machine. It is from Peter Dalgliesh, a British colleague who works for Best Securicor Guarding in England.

The address is
Best Securicor Guarding
Head Office
Sutton Park House
15 Carshalton Road
Sutton
Surrey SM1 4LD
Phone: 020 - 87707000
Fax: 020 - 87222530

Peter has heard of the international fair 'Security' at the Messe in Essen. European companies will be represented. They will demonstrate sophisticated techniques. They will organize workshops on these issues. The event has to take place on October 5,6 and 7.

Peter likes:
• to visit the fair in Essen
• to visit the branch office in Essen
• to discuss ideas on exchanging personnel

Your manager decides to send back a fax message.
He asks you to fill in the first page.

Faxbericht

AN/TO _____

z.Hd. / ATTN _____

FAXNR. _____

BETRIFFT/CONCERNING _____

_____

_____

DATUM/DATE _____

SEITENANZAHL/NR.OF PAGES _____
INKL. DIESE SEITE/THIS PAGE

VON/FROM _____
FAX.NR _____
NAME _____
ABTEILUNG/DEPARTMENT _____

Sollten Sie dieses Fax unvollständig empfangen haben, nehmen Sie
bitte Kontakt auf mit
If this fax has been received incomplete or illegible please contact

Best - Sec Essen
Markelplatz 17
42166 Essen
Telefon: 0049 (0)201 - 3789310
Telefax: 0049 (0)201 - 4437845

Track 44

Task 14

Today you are at the reception of your company, Best-Sec. It's ten o'clock in the morning when a call of a colleague, Ellen Cowley, from the office in Liverpool comes in.

Work in pairs. Work out the dialogue.
Fill in the blanks. Switch roles. Check by listening to the dialogue.

large-scale contract	Großauftrag
offer	Angebot
in advance	im voraus
effort	Mühe
memo	Mitteilung, Notiz

Security Rex:

Sie melden sich mit Ihrem eigenen Namen und dem Namen der Firma.

Sie bestätigen dies.

Sie sagen, dass es Ihnen Leid tut, aber ihr Chef z. Zt. in einer Besprechung sitzt und erst gegen 13.30 Uhr wieder erreichbar ist.

Machen Sie das Angebot, Herrn Kasper in der Mittagspause gegen 11.30 Uhr um einen Rückruf zu bitten.

Sie verneinen und bitten um Angabe der Telefonnummer.

Ellen Cowley:

Sie stellen sich vor und fragen, ob der Rezeptionist Englisch spricht.

Sie bitten darum, mit dem Abteilungsleiter, Herrn Kasper, verbunden zu werden.

Teilen Sie ihm mit, dass es sehr dringend ist, da es sich um einen Großauftrag bei einem Ihrer wichtigsten amerikanischen Kunden handelt.

Sie sind einverstanden und fragen, ob der Rezeptionist Ihre Nummer hat.

Die Nummer lautet 0033 - 4- 568933.

Sie wiederholen 0033 - 4 - 568933.

Sie bestätigen die Nummer und verabschieden sich im voraus mit Dank für
die Mühe.

Sie sagen 'Keine Ursache' und
beenden das Gespräch.

Now make a telephone memo in English for the head of the department.

10 11 12 1 2 Datum	**Telefonnotiz**
9 Uhrzeit 3	
8 7 6 5 4	

An

Anruf von

☐ ruft wieder an   am / um

☐ bittet um Kontakt ✆ Nr.

Aufgenommen von:

Erledigt durch   Datum
☐ Anruf
☐ Brief   Zchn.
☐ Besuch

Telefonnotiz 1019

Zweckform

At the stadium – checking and describing persons

Ein häufiges Einsatzgebiet für die Schutz- und Sicherheitskraft sind auch Stadien, wo nicht mehr nur Fußballspiele ausgetragen werden, sondern auch andere sportliche Großveranstaltungen, aber auch Konzerte, Opern und Parties stattfinden, an denen zunehmend internationale Kunden und deren Mitarbeiter teilnehmen.

Die Tätigkeiten zur Gewährleistung der Sicherheit von Personen und Objekten umfassen u. a. die Ermittlung der Konflikt- und Gefährdungspotenziale, Dokumentation der Maßnahmen und eventueller Vorfälle, Durchführung von Zugangskontrollen, Kommunikation mit öffentlichen Institutionen wie Polizei, Feuerwehr, anderen Sicherheitsdiensten u. v. m.

In Konfliktsituationen müssen Sie deeskalierend wirken, im Gefahrenfall Anweisungen geben können und zur Gefahrprävention möglicherweise auch Personenbeschreibungen weiterleiten.

In diesem Teil lernen Sie, o.g. Tätigkeiten in der englischen Sprache zu bewältigen.

stadium regulations	Stadionordnung
operator	Betreiber, Inhaber
to appoint	einsetzen
to gather	sammeln
premises	Gelände

Event

You are working for a security team at a stadium in Germany. Your first task is to gather some information and to get to know the stadium regulations given to you by the operator.

Later you are appointed in various functions around the stadium to guarantee security for people and the premises.

Task 1

to be entitled	berechtigt sein
admission	Zugang
in possession of	in Besitz von
valid	gültig
to grant	gestatten
entitlement	Berechtigung
to enter	betreten
means	Mittel
to take place	stattfinden
ancillary facilities	Nebeneinrichtungen
occasion	Anlass, Gelegenheit
event	Veranstaltung
visitor	Besucher
to be obliged to	verpflichtet sein zu etw.
to present	vorlegen
stewarding service	Kontrolldienst
to surrender	aushändigen
on request	auf Anfrage
nationwide	national
banning	Verbot
to attend	teilnehmen
to turn s.o. away	jmd. zurückweisen
to eject	verweisen
to encounter	antreffen

Read the text.

A Persons entitled to admission
Only those persons who are in possession of a valid ticket or other type of pass granting admission to the stadium or who are able to demonstrate their entitlement to enter by some other means or who are able to demonstrate by other means their entitlement to enter on days on which no event is taking place are entitled to enter the stadium and the ancillary facilities.

B Entry checks

1. Upon entering the stadium on the occasion of an event all visitors are obliged to present their tickets or passes without being asked to the stadium's stewarding and security service or the police and to surrender said tickets or passes for inspection on request.
2. Visitors who are unable to demonstrate their entitlement to enter the stadium or who have received a local or nationwide banning order preventing them from attending sporting events or any other type of event are not permitted to enter the stadium. They will be turned away by the stadium's stewarding and security service or the police or ejected from the stadium if they are encountered there.

Write down whether the following statements are true or false.

	T	F
1. Only visitors in possession of tickets are allowed to enter the stadium.		
2. If you want to enter the stadium you have to present the ticket without being asked.		
3. On days on which no event is taking place nobody can't get into the stadium.		
4. Tickets have to be presented to the stadium's stewarding and security service and the police.		
5. Visitors who haven't got a valid ticket may get admission by presenting another pass that entitles them to enter the stadium.		
6. Visitors who haven't got a ticket or pass are not permitted to enter the stadium.		
7. Only the police is allowed to eject persons who have received a banning from the stadium.		
8. People who received a nationwide banning from attending sporting events may enter the stadium for concerts.		

Task 2

Match the definitions with expressions from the text. What is the password?

1. act of coming or going in
2. performing duties, e.g. working for a company
3. incident connected with sport
4. enclosed area of land for games
5. official organization whose job is to keep public order, prevent and solve crime
6. belonging to a particular place or district
7. incident
8. printed piece of card that entitles the holder to enter the stadium
9. meet or find oneself faced by somebody
10. officially forbidding
11. entering or being allowed to enter a building

Password:................................

67

entry ticket	Eintrittskarte
season ticket	Dauerkarte
mobile (phone)	Handy
to switch off	ausschalten

Task 3

You're at the entrance of the stadium checking the entry tickets.
Work out the dialogue with your partner. Switch roles.

Excuse me, can I have a look at your ticket?

Sorry, but I can't find it. But believe me I've got a season ticket. I'm here with the fan club.

Sagen Sie, es tut Ihnen leid, aber ohne Eintrittskarte können Sie den Fan nicht in das Stadion lassen.

Look, that's my season ticket from last year!

Sagen Sie, es ist nicht gültig und bitten Sie den Fan zur Seite zu treten und noch mal gründlich das Ticket zu suchen.

May I go inside to look for my friend? Maybe he's got it.

Sagen Sie, dass Sie ihn abweisen müssen. Er soll versuchen, seinen Freund per Handy anzurufen.

That's a good idea. I just hope he hasn't got his mobile switched off.

Task 4

You're at the access control of the stadium. A German team plays a British one in the UEFA-Cup.
Fans come in and have to be checked for prohibited items.
A British fan with a big rucksack who seems to have been drinking already, approaches the access control.

access control	Zugangskontrolle
item	Gegenstand
to approach	sich nähern

Listen to the conversation.

Track 45

Task 5

bottle	Flasche
to joke	scherzen
previous	früher
experience	Erfahrung

Now read the pieces of the conversation. It is all mixed up. Find out what comes first and what comes next.
Use figures 1 to 6 and make them correspond by putting them in the appropriate boxes. The first one has already been done for you. Check your answers with the conversation.

68

The security
officer says:

to prohibit	verbieten
beverage	Getränk
to dispose of	entsorgen
litter-bin	Abfalleimer
belongings	Wertsachen

☐ • I'm sorry, but resulting from previous experience the organizers of the match have prohibited the sale and consumption of any kind of alcoholic drink in the stadium.

☐ • As I told you. No alcoholic beverages in the stadium. That means you'll either have to leave the rucksack in your car or you dispose of the bottles into one of the litter-bins next to the entrance.

☐ • Thanks. Enjoy the match.

☐ • Well, I have to tell you that you aren't allowed to take any alcoholic drinks into the stadium.

☐ • Good afternoon. Excuse me, what have you got in that bag?

☐ • Okay. What you could also do is to go over to one of those orange coloured containers. You can leave your bag over there and they'll look after your belongings for as long as the match.

The fan says:

1   What! Are you joking? And this country has the reputation of being the beer-drinking country!
2   Forget it! I don't own a car.
3   Only some bottles of beer.
4   All right. I knew you Germans were perfectly organized.
5   I can't believe it! And what am I going to do now?

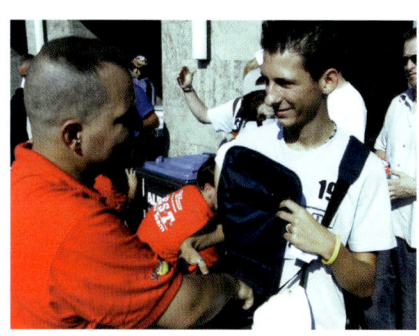

Task 6

Use the English expressions mentioned above. Write them down.

1. Was haben Sie in Ihrer Tasche?
2. Sie sind nicht berechtigt, alkoholische Getränke mit ins Stadion zu nehmen.
3. Sie machen wohl Scherze!
4. Die Organisatoren haben den Verkauf und Konsum von alkoholischen Getränken verboten.
5. Alkoholische Getränke sind im Stadion verboten.
6. Entsorgen Sie die Flaschen in einem der Abfalleimer.
7. Vergessen Sie's!
8. Sie können Ihre Tasche dort zur Aufbewahrung abgeben.
9. Sie werden auf ihre Wertsachen aufpassen.
10. Viel Spaß beim Spiel.

1. ....
2. ....
    ....
3. ....
4. ....
    ....
5. ....
6. ....
7. ....
8. ....
9. ....
10. ....

Task 7

prohibited	verboten
can	Dose
caustic	ätzend
dyestuff	Färbemittel
pressurised	druckbeaufschlagt
brittle	zerbrechlich
splittering	splitternd
bulky	sperrig
flare	Fackel
pole	Stange
banner	Transparent
xenophobic	fremden-, ausländerfeindlich

For safety reasons there are several prohibited items that visitors entering the area covered by the stadium regulations are not allowed to bring into the stadium.

Read the following list of prohibited items and categorize them. Use the table below. Some might belong to more than one category

- weapons
- gas spray cans
- perfume bottle
- caustic substances
- dyestuffs
- pressurised containers for gases
- pocket cigarette lighters
- containers made from brittle or splintering material
- bulky objects such as stools or suitcases
- fireworks, rockets, hand-held flares, smoke powder, signal rockets and other pyrotechnic objects
- poles for flags or banners that are not made of wood or are longer than 2 m or more than 3 cm in diameter
- large banners, large quantities of paper, wallpaper
- mechanically and electrically operated instruments
- alcoholic drinks with an alcohol content of more than 15% by volume and drugs
- animals
- racist, xenophobic and radical material

items which could be thrown	items that can make noise	items which could cause injuries	items which are inflammable

Task 8

On the premises of the stadium you work together with fan coaches who make sure that no banned fans enter the stadium. On your patrol before the match you believe to recognise a fan from Holland who was denied entering the stadium last season.

You take out your wireless set and get into contact with Gerrit who's a Dutch fan coacher.

to harass	belästigen
lad	Typ
stand-by	auf Empfang bleiben

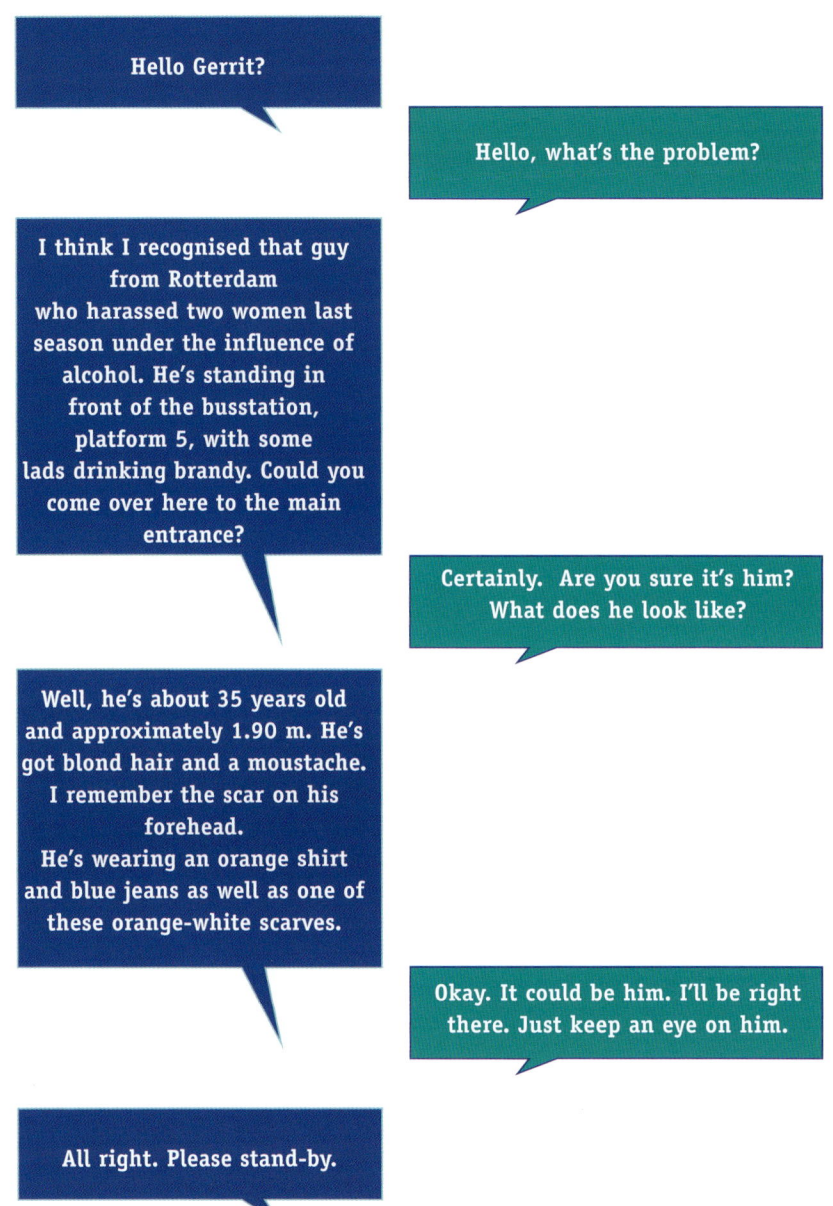

Hello Gerrit?

Hello, what's the problem?

I think I recognised that guy from Rotterdam who harassed two women last season under the influence of alcohol. He's standing in front of the busstation, platform 5, with some lads drinking brandy. Could you come over here to the main entrance?

Certainly. Are you sure it's him? What does he look like?

Well, he's about 35 years old and approximately 1.90 m. He's got blond hair and a moustache. I remember the scar on his forehead. He's wearing an orange shirt and blue jeans as well as one of these orange-white scarves.

Okay. It could be him. I'll be right there. Just keep an eye on him.

All right. Please stand-by.

Answer the following questions:
1. Where is the fan and what is he doing?
2. How did the safety and security specialist recognise the banned fan?
3. What does the fan coacher do?

71

Track 45

Task 9

Study the conversation in task 4 again. Work out the following dialogue. Work with a partner.

You are still on duty on the premises outside the stadium. You are calling a Spanish fan coacher on the wireless.

stand	Stand
to smash	zerschlagen
car park	Parkplatz
scene	Ort des Geschehens

Hello Antonio?

Hello, this is Antonio?

Sagen Sie, dass es Probleme mit zwei spanischen Hooligans gibt.

What's up?

Sagen Sie, dass die Fans unter Alkoholeinfluss stehen und bereits zwei Tische an einem Bierstand beim Busparkplatz zerschlagen haben.

Okay, I'm on my way but it'll take me 10 minutes to arrive at the scene.

Sagen Sie, Sie werden warten und mit einem Kollegen versuchen, die beiden Hooligans zu beruhigen.

Task 10

Persons who are wanted or missing can often be traced with the help of a description.
If you detected a person try to remember as many details as you can.
Here are some expressions for describing people in English. Learn them by heart.

name	Name
first name	Vorname
last name	Nachname
nickname	Spitzname
age	Alter
exact age	genaues Alter
approximate age	ungefähres Alter

72

appearance	Erscheinung
height	Größe
build (thin, slim, stout)	Gestalt (dünn, schlank, beleibt)
head (large, small)	Kopf (groß, klein)
face (round, long, wrinkled)	Gesicht (rund, lang, faltig)
hair (colour, bald, unkempt, curly, beard, moustache)	Haar (Farbe, glatzköpfig, ungekämmt, lockig, Bart, Schnurrbart)
forehead	Stirn
eyebrows (thick, thin, plucked)	Augenbrauen (dick, dünn, gezupft)
eyes (colour, glasses)	Augen (Farbe, Brille)
nose (long, short)	Nase (lang, kurz)
mouth (large, small)	Mund (groß, klein)
lips (thin, thick)	Lippen (dünn, dick)
teeth	Zähne
chin (protruding)	Kinn (vorstehend)
ears	Ohren

Now describe one of your fellow students in front of the class. Let them guess who it is.

Task 11

You're still standing on patrol near the bus- and tramstation. A woman is coming over to you.
Read the following conversation with your partner. Switch roles.

tram	Straßenbahn
packed	brechend voll
to be torn apart	auseinander gerissen werden
meeting point	Treffpunkt
by radio	über Funk
to page	ausrufen

Excuse me, madam. Do you speak English?

Certainly. Can I help you?

My name is Andrea Lorenzo. I'm from Italy. I can't find my son!

Where and when did you last see him?

We were stepping out of one of the trams. It was packed with people. I was holding his hand then but we were torn apart and suddenly I couldn't see him anymore.

73

What does your son look like?

He's 10 years old. He's got dark hair and he's got brown eyes. He's quite heavy for his age with a round face.

What is he wearing?

Blue Jeans, a sweater and a football scarf.

Well, madam. I suggest you walk up to the meeting point just next to the stadium's shop. There's a sign saying 'THW' that stands for 'Technisches Hilfswerk'. Everything will be taken care of. I'll see to it at once.

Thank you so much!

What's his name again?

It's Roberto.

Roberto Lorenzo. Does he speak English?

No, I'm sorry.

OK. I'll ask them by radio to page him in Italian. Don't worry.

Task 12

Now work with your partner. Imagine you were at a concert and you lost your best friend. Your partner appears in the role of a safety and security specialist. Play the roles and take turns.

Task 13

Listen to the conversation.

Track 46   Listen to the dialogue again and write down the used English expressions:

1. Entschuldigung?...
2. Sprechen Sie Englisch? ....
3. Kann ich Ihnen helfen? ....

4. Haben Sie schon ein Ticket? ....
5. Gehen Sie geradeaus. ....
6. Neben Sie den Nordeingang auf der linken Seite. ....
   ....
7. Folgen Sie der Beschilderung. ....
8. Sie sitzen in der neunten Reihe, Platz Nr. 14 ....
9. Danke für Ihre Hilfe. ....
10. Keine Ursache. ....

sticker	Aufkleber
aluminium	Aluminium
up to	bis
plastic	Kunststoff
mix-up	Verwechslung

Task 14

Translate the following situation into English (S.a.s.s. = safety and security specialist):

S.a.s.s.	Entschuldigung bitte. Darf ich bitte mal in Ihre Tasche schauen?
Fan	Entschuldigung, ich spreche kein Deutsch. Sprechen Sie Englisch?
S.a.s.s.	Ja, natürlich. Darf ich bitte mal in Ihre Tasche schauen?
Fan	Ich habe keine verbotenen Gegenstände dabei.
S.a.s.s.	Was ist das?
Fan	Das ist meine Getränkeflasche.
S.a.s.s.	Tut mir leid, aber das ist eine Aluminiumflasche und darf nicht mit ins Stadion genommen werden.
Fan	Aber die ist doch unzerbrechlich.
S.a.s.s.	Das ist richtig. Aber Sie könnten diese auf das Spielfeld werfen und jemanden verletzen.
Fan	Darf man keine Getränke mit in das Stadion nehmen?
S.a.s.s.	Erlaubt sind Getränke bis 0,5 l in Kunststoffflaschen.
Fan	Das hätte man vorher wissen müssen.
S.a.s.s.	Tut mir leid. Gehen Sie am besten zu dem roten Container und geben Sie Ihre Flasche dort ab.
Fan	Kann ich sicher gehen, dass ich meine Flasche zurückerhalte bei 50.000 Besuchern hier?
S.a.s.s.	Da sehe ich kein Problem. Die Flasche und Ihr Ticket erhalten jeweils einen Aufkleber mit einer Nummer, so dass keine Verwechslung möglich ist.

Task 15

How to say in German? Match the sentences 1-10 with the appropriate German sentences a-j. The first has already been done for you.

to allocate	zuweisen

1. The fact that I'm only doing my job here doesn't give you the right to insult me.

2. Well, I've had enough now. You can't go into the stadium.

3. That goes for you, too!

4. You just calm down.

5. When you buy a ticket, you accept all the rules that apply in and around the stadium.

6. Let's try to sort things out.

7. You may only occupy your allocated seat.

75

8. I'm looking for the nearest cashpoint and a cigarette machine.

9. All access stairways and emergency exits must be kept clear at all times.

10. Who started the fight?

a.   Beruhigen Sie sich.
b.   Und das gilt auch für Sie!
c.   Alle Auf- und Abgänge sowie Rettungswege sind uneingeschränkt freizuhalten.
d.   Die Tatsache, dass ich hier nur meinen Job mache, gibt Ihnen nicht das Recht, mich zu beleidigen.
e.   Lassen Sie uns eine Lösung finden.
f.   Sie dürfen nur auf dem Ihnen zugewiesenen Platz sitzen.
g.   So, jetzt habe ich genug. Sie dürfen nicht ins Stadion.
h.   Wer hat mit der Schlägerei angefangen?
i.   Mit dem Kauf einer Eintrittskarte akzeptieren Sie alle Bedingungen, die im und um das Stadion gelten.
j.   Ich suche den nächsten Geld- und Zigarettenautomaten.

1	2	3	4	5	6	7	8	9	10
d									

08//

At the store

In den letzten Jahrzehnten hat die Zahl der Ladendiebstähle stetig zugenommen.

Die Eigentümer von Kauf- und Warenhäusern haben verschie-dene Maßnahmen ergriffen, u. a. durch den Einsatz von Ladendetektiven, um die Zahl der Diebstähle zu reduzieren. Zu diesem Zweck werden auch die Schutz- und Sicherheitskräfte eingesetzt.

In diesem Kapitel werden Begriffe und Redewendungen behandelt, die für einen Ladendetektiv von Bedeutung sind.

Task 1

You are hired as a store detective in a department store. You inform yourself about the store's methods to prevent shoplifting.

Match the methods to the pictures:

to hire	einstellen
store detective	Ladendetektiv
department store	Kaufhaus

electronic tag	Diebstahlsicherung, Schild
wire	Draht
goods	Güter, Waren
display cabinet	Schaukasten
out of reach	außer Reichweite
video surveillance	Videoüberwachung
CCTV	Kameraüberwachung
to track	verfolgen
mirror	Spiegel

- fixing electronic tags to articles
- customer observance
- locking goods away in a display cabinet
- putting articles out of reach
- using video surveillance - fixing CCTV (closed-circuit TV) cameras at strategic points to track customers

Task 2

Track 47

A shoplifter. Listen to the conversation. Tick the appropriate box.

to be caught	gefasst werden
to wear	tragen
fur	Pelz
queue	Schlange
to gather	zusammenpacken
crisps	Chips
to faint	ohnmächtig werden
ill	krank
worth	im Wert von

	T	F
1. Jane works in the shoe department.		
2. They caught the shoplifter yesterday.		
3. The lady was wearing a fur coat.		
4. There was a long queue.		
5. The woman couldn't find her credit card.		
6. She gathered her goods quickly.		
7. The lady fell on the floor.		
8. The lady had stolen a packet of crisps.		
9. She fainted because she was ill.		
10. She had stolen at least 30 pounds worth of goods.		

Task 3

Track 48

Listen to the conversation.

Task 4

Track 48

Now listen to the conversation of task 3 again. Then read it. Match the German sentences 1 to 10 with sentences used in the dialogue. Check your answers.

Shop assistant:	Excuse me, Madam. We have reason to believe that you took articles from the shop without paying.
Shoplifter:	I beg your pardon? Why should I take things from your shop? I'm a well-to-do citizen of this city and I live in great luxury.
Shop assistant:	I'm sorry, but we saw on our camera that you put two bottles of perfume in your coat. I think it would be very wise if you didn't make a fuss here and just follow us to the office. Then we will call the police and the matter will be settled.
Shoplifter:	Oh please, don't do that to me! My good name will be in the newspaper. I can't have that!
Shop assistant:	Again I'm sorry. We have reasons to believe that you have been shoplifting before in our shop.
Shoplifter:	This is so embarrassing. Can't we settle this matter, please?
Shop assistant:	If we had to do that with all shoplifters, there wouldn't be much time left for us to help honest customers.

reason	Grund
to believe	glauben
articles	Artikel
without	ohne
well-to-do	reich
citizen	Bürger
bottle	Flasche
to make a fuss	Aufheben um etwas machen
to settle the matter	die Angelegenheit regeln
(news)paper	Zeitung
honest	ehrlich
customer	Kunde

1. Das ist so peinlich.
2. Wie bitte?
3. Folgen Sie uns in das Büro.
4. Sie haben zwei Parfumflaschen in Ihren Mantel gesteckt.
5. Wir haben Gründe anzunehmen, dass Sie Artikel aus dem Geschäft mitgenommen haben, ohne sie zu bezahlen.
6. Wir sahen auf unserer Kamera, dass...
7. Es ist vernünftiger, hier nicht so ein Aufheben zu machen.
8. Wir werden die Polizei anrufen und die Sache wird geregelt werden.
9. Wir haben Gründe zu glauben, dass Sie schon früher in unserem Geschäft gestohlen haben.
10. Es würde nicht viel Zeit überbleiben, um ehrlichen Kunden zu helfen.

Task 5

Work out the dialogue with your partner. Switch roles.

Shoplifter	Shop assistant

Bitten Sie den Herrn um Entschuldigung. Teilen Sie ihm mit, dass Sie Grund haben anzunehmen, dass er Artikel aus dem Geschäft entwendet hat, ohne zu bezahlen.

Drücken Sie Ihr Entsetzen aus und fragen Sie, warum Sie Grund haben sollten, Dinge aus dem Laden zu entwenden.

Teilen Sie ihm mit, es täte Ihnen Leid. Sie hätten per Kamera beobachtet, dass er eine Flasche in seine Tasche gesteckt hat.

Sagen Sie, Sie hätten genug Geld und müssen nicht stehlen.

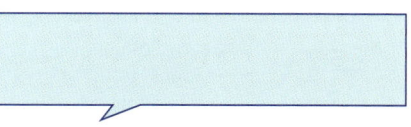

79

Bitten Sie den Ladendieb, Ihnen ins Büro zu folgen, um kein Aufsehen zu erregen.

Fragen Sie den Ladendetektiv, ob die Polizei gerufen wird.

Bestätigen Sie dies und sagen Sie, dass dann die Angelegenheit geregelt wird.

Sagen Sie, dass es wohl weiser wäre, mit zu gehen.

Stimmen Sie ihm zu und fragen Sie ihn, ob er früher schon einmal einen Ladendiebstahl begangen hat.

Verneinen Sie dies und sagen Sie, dass es Ihnen sehr peinlich ist.

Task 6

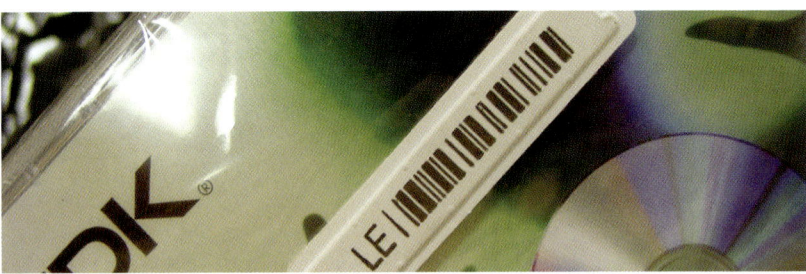

You are a store detective in the electronics department of a big store in Frankfurt and have just observed a customer putting a discman into his coat pocket.
You approach him when he is about to leave the store.

Work out this dialogue. Work with a partner and practise your dialogue. Switch roles.

to observe	beobachten
to approach	ansprechen
to witness	bezeugen, mit ansehen
to be mistaken	im Irrtum sein
receipt	Kassenbon
to empty	leeren
to search	durchsuchen

Entschuldigung. Würden Sie bitte mit mir kommen?

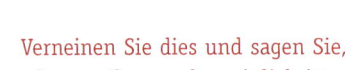

Sorry, I don't speak any German.

Teilen Sie ihm auf Englisch mit, dass Sie Ladendetektiv sind und bitten Sie ihn, mit Ihnen zu kommen.

What do you want from me? I paid for everything!

80

Sagen Sie, dass Sie ihm das gleich in Ihrem Büro und nicht vor Kunden erläutern werden.

I don't know what this is all about.

Sagen Sie, dass Sie ihm bei einem Diebstahl beobachtet haben.

You must be mistaken. I've just bought two CD's. Here's the receipt.

Bitten Sie ihn, Ihnen den Inhalt seiner Jackentasche zu leeren.

No, I won't.

Teilen Sie ihm mit, dass Sie nun die Polizei rufen werden, da Sie nicht befugt sind, ihn zu durchsuchen, und bitten Sie ihn, Platz zu nehmen.

Now listen to the conversation. Compare it with your version.

Track 49

Task 7

You are now working as a store detective in the food department of the store in the basement. You stop a teenager just leaving the cashier.

Work out this dialogue as you did in Task 6.

possibly	möglicherweise
to forget	vergessen
cash desk	Kasse

Entschuldigung, bleiben Sie bitte stehen.

Sorry, I don't understand.

Stellen Sie sich in Englisch als Ladendetektiv vor. Fragen Sie ihn, ob es sein könnte, dass er vergessen hat, etwas an der Kasse zu bezahlen.

81

to hide	verstecken
brandy	Kognak
to confess	gestehen, zugeben
sensitive	vernünftig
ID card	Personalausweis
statement	Aussage, Stellungnahme
particulars	Personalien

Fragen Sie ihn, ob er die Videokamera sieht und teilen Sie ihm mit, dass mit dem Überwachungssystem beobachtet wurde, wie er eine Flasche Kognak unter seiner Jacke versteckte.

No, you must be mistaken.

Sagen Sie ihm, dass es sehr vernünftig ist. Fragen Sie ihn, ob er sich ausweisen kann.

Well, I think it would be better to confess. Yes, I took a bottle. I'm sorry. There you are.

Teilen Sie ihm mit, dass er mit in Ihr Büro kommen muss, um die Stellungnahme und Personalien aufzunehmen.

Yes, I'm British. Shall I give it to you now?

All right.

Task 8

Track 50

Now listen to the conversation. Compare it with your version.

Task 9

As a safety and security specialist you have to be up-to-date when it comes to the latest developments in the security business. In one of the foreign magazines you spot an article about preventing shoplifting.

Read the text

Let's imagine for the moment that you own a big department store and you are having a big problem with shoplifting. What are you going to do? You cannot let it continue, because every month your accounting system tells you that you are losing thousands of euros to theft. It forces you to raise prices, and that means you have to charge more than the store next door. That can make it very hard to compete, especially if the store next door is successfully discouraging shoplifting.

As a retailer focusing on the problem of what's known in the industry as loss prevention, you basically have three methods at your disposal to slow the shoplifters down:
(1) You can watch everyone in the store like a hawk and make sure they don't steal anything. You can do that using safety and security specialists and/or video surveillance systems;
(2) You can make things hard to remove from the store by bolting them down, attaching wires, putting things in display cabinets and behind the counter;
(3) You can use a system that attaches special tags onto everything so that an alarm goes off whenever a shoplifter tries to walk out with an item.

department store	Kaufhaus
accounting system	Buchführungs-, Abrechnungssystem
theft	Diebstahl
to force	zwingen
to discourage	abschrecken, entmutigen
loss prevention	Schadenverhütung
disposal	Verfügung
hawk	Falke
to bolt	verschrauben
electronic	elektronische
article surveillance	Artikelüberwachung
unbeatable	unschlagbar
to enable	ermöglichen

Security experts say the most effective anti-shoplifting tools these days are CCTV and tag-and-alarm systems. These systems are better known as electronic article surveillance (EAS) systems. Used separately, these are good options. Used together, experts say, they're almost unbeatable. EAS is a technology used to identify articles as they pass through a gated area in a store. This identification is used to alert someone that unauthorized removal of items is being attempted. EAS systems are useful in any situation where there is an opportunity for theft of items of any size. Using an EAS system enables the retailer to display popular items on the floor, where they can be seen, rather than putting them in locked cabinets or behind the counter.

Task 10

Now tick the appropriate box whether the statements are true or false.

	T	F
1. As a retailer you are losing thousands of euros to theft if you don't invest in loss prevention		
2. If you successfully discourage shoplifting you find it easier to compete with other retailers		
3. There are four methods to prevent shoplifting		
4. One method to prevent shoplifting is to put things behind the cashier		
5. You can watch customers with special tags attached to articles		
6. Today the most effective anti-shoplifting tool is CCTV		
7. CCTV doesn't work along with EAS		
8. To use EAS the store must have gates		
9. With EAS you can detect items of all sizes		
10. With EAS you don't have to lock articles in display cabinets		

83

Task 11

How to say in German?

1. It forces you to raise prices.
2. Installing an EAS is a means of loss prevention.
3. Video surveillance systems are successfully discouraging shoplifting.
4. Items are put in display cabinets and behind the counter.
5. Special tags are attached to items so that an alarm goes off.
6. Attaching tags to clothes belongs to the electronic article surveillance (EAS)systems.
7. Together, CCTV and EAS are unbeatable.
8. It identifies articles as they pass through a gated area.
9. There is an opportunity for theft of items of any size.
10. An EAS system enables the retailer to display items on the floor.

At the airport

Terrorismus ist bereits seit den 70er Jahren ein Problem für Fluglinien. Flugzeugentführungen und Sprengstoffanschläge wurden auf der ganzen Welt zu Methoden subversiver und militanter Organisationen. Obwohl die Sicherheitskontrollen auf Flughäfen immer schon streng waren, haben die Anschläge vom 11. September 2001 vielen Menschen aufgezeigt, dass sie nicht vorsichtig genug waren.

Bei ca. jährlich 730 Millionen Flugreisenden weltweit muss ausreichende Sicherheit gewährleistet werden, die an Flughäfen u. a. auch durch Sicherheitsdienstleistungsunternehmen übernommen wird. Dabei kann es gerade im Kontroll- und Sicherheitsbereich zu verschiedenen Situationen kommen, in denen Sie in der Fremdsprache Englisch mit Passagieren kommunizieren müssen.

Event

You belong to Security staff at the Frankfurt Airport. Today you are working at the access control in the security area. You switch functions with one of your colleagues and either search people with the metal detector or sit at the screen for checking the passengers' luggage for suspicious items.

Task 1

A man just passed through the metal detection gate and it beeped. You start talking to the man.
Listen to the conversation. Then read the text with your partner. Switch roles.

Track 51

security area	Sicherheitsbereich
to search	durchsuchen
metal detection gate	Torsonde

screen	Bildschirm
luggage	Gepäck
suspicious	verdächtig
item	Gegenstand
hand detector	Handsonde
to beep	piepsen, ein akkustisches Signal geben
to take off	ausziehen
definitely	bestimmt
federal police	Bundespolizei
to trigger	auslösen

Entschuldigung. Der Metalldetektor hat gerade gepiepst. Haben Sie auch alle Metallgegenstände abgelegt?

Sorry, I don't speak German.

Sorry. I didn't know you were English. Did you really take all metal items off your person?

Yes, I certainly did.

When I used the hand detector it beeped at your shoes. Would you be so kind as to take your shoes off?

No, definitely not.

I'm afraid, sir, that I'll have to ask you to follow me to the federal police to search you in the room on the left.

All right. There's nothing in my shoes. Something else must have triggered the alarm.

Task 2

Read the following conversation (S.a.s.s. = safety and security specialist):

belt	Gürtel
to take off	ablegen
X-ray machine	Röntgengerät
to hide	verstecken
razor blade	Rasierklinge
ridiculous	lächerlich
to eliminate	ausschließen
possibility	Möglichkeit
danger	Gefahr
current	aktuell, jüngste/r
event	Ereignis

S.a.s.s.	Entschuldigung. Würden Sie bitte den Gürtel ablegen?
Passenger	Do you speak English?
S.a.s.s.	Yes, I do. Would you take off the belt, please?
Passenger	Yes, sure. Is something wrong with it?
S.a.s.s.	We'll see after it's been taken through the X-ray machine.
Passenger	All right.
S.a.s.s.	Okay, there's your belt.

Passenger	Thanks. What should I hide in a belt anyway?
S.a.s.s.	Well, you may easily hide a razor blade in it!
Passenger	That's ridiculous!
S.a.s.s.	We have to eliminate all possibility of danger. Due to current events we have to take into account everything. Safety first!
Passenger	You're right. Good bye.
S.a.s.s.	Good bye. Enjoy your flight.

Now listen to the text. Write down the used expressions.

Track 52

1. Wir haben jedes Gefahrenpotential auszuschließen.
   ....

2. Würden Sie bitte den Gürtel abnehmen?
   ....

3. Sie könnten leicht eine Rasierklinge darin verstecken.
   ....

4. Das werden wir sehen, wenn es durch die Gepäckprüfanlage gelaufen ist.
   ....

5. Guten Flug!
   ....

6. Ist damit etwas nicht in Ordnung?
   ....

7. Das ist ja lächerlich!
   ....

8. Wir müssen alles in Betracht ziehen.
   ....

9. Hier haben Sie Ihren Gürtel zurück.
   ....

10. Aufgrund aktueller Ereignisse.
    ....

Task 3

hand luggage	Handgepäck
bulk baggage	Reisegepäck
luggage	Gepäck
baggage	Gepäck
accidentally	versehentlich
nailscissors	Nagelschere
Swiss army knife	Schweizer Messer
instruction	Anweisung
coin	Münze
tray	Tablett
gift	Geschenk
no longer	nicht mehr

Read the following text. Then complete the conversation. Work with a partner. Take turns.

What can you do when you have accidentally packed your (nail)scissors, your Swiss army knife or some other item that you are not allowed to take with you in your hand luggage* or when security staff decides that an item is potentially dangerous?

- Put the item in your bulk baggage before you check in.
- Hand it in to the security staff.
- Go to one of the service points and pay to have it sent on by post. However it is not possible to do so in the case of security checks at the gate.

You should follow the instructions of the security staff at all times.

Safety and security specialist: Passenger:

Bitten Sie den Passagier, alle metallischen Gegenstände, Ihre Schlüssel, Münzen, ihr Handy etc. auf das Tablett zu legen?

Bestätigen Sie. Teilen Sie der Sicherheitskraft mit, dass Sie vergessen haben, ihre Nagelschere und ihr Schweizer Messer in das Reisegepäck zu packen.

Teilen Sie dem Passagier mit, dass er beides im Abfalleimer neben der Torsonde entsorgen soll.

Sagen Sie, dass es sich bei dem Schweizer Messer um ein persönliches Geschenk handelt. Sie möchten die Gegenstände nach Hause schicken.

Sagen Sie, dass dies ist hier am Sicherheitscheck nicht mehr möglich ist.

Sagen Sie, dass Sie sich den Anweisungen des Sicherheitspersonals fügen müssen.

Bedanken Sie sich und wünschen Sie einen guten Flug.

*   Gepäck kann im Englischen übersetzt werden mit luggage oder baggage. In der Luftfahrt, vor allem im amerikanischen Raum, ist häufiger der Begriff baggage anzutreffen (z. B. baggage claim = Gepäckausgabe). Damit werden gewöhnlich größere Gepäckstücke bezeichnet.

Task 4

Now listen to the conversation in English. Compare it with your version.

Track 53

Task 5

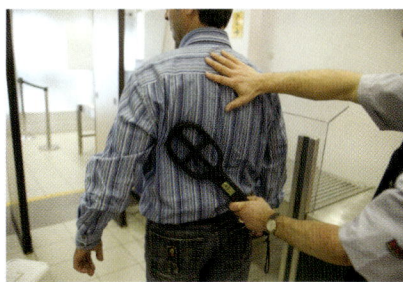

gun	Waffe
knife	Messer
bag	Tasche
litter bin	Abfalleimer
conveyor belt	Fließband
gate detector	Torsonde
auch:	
metal detector	Torsonde
X-ray radiation	Röntgenstrahlung
possession	Besitz
to damage	beschädigen

Match the sentences 1 to 10 with the sentences in a – j which have the same meaning.
The first one has already been done for you.

1. Würden Sie bitte Ihre Hosentasche leeren?
2. Sie können Ihr Messer gegen ein Entgeld in unserem Fundbüro hinterlegen.
3. Bitte entsorgen Sie Ihr Messer im Abfalleimer.
4. Bitte gehen Sie durch die Torsonde.
5. Bitte legen Sie alle Gegenstände auf das Band.
6. Legen Sie auch Ihre Jacken und die Kamera auf das Förderband.
7. Die Strahlung ist nicht hoch genug, dass Sie Ihre Filme zerstört.
8. Alle Gegenstände müssen die Gepäckprüfanlage durchlaufen.
9. War Ihr Gepäck stets unter Ihrer Aufsicht?
10. Sie werden durch einen Sicherheitsbeamten durchsucht.

a. All items must go through an X-ray machine.
b. X-ray radiation is not high enough to damage photographic films.
c. You can deposit your knife for a consideration in our lost property office.
d. Would you dispose of your knife into the litter bin, please?
e. Please walk through the gate detector.
f. Has your luggage been in your possession at all times?

89

g. Place the jacket and the camera onto the conveyor belt, too.
h. Would you be so kind as to empty the trouser pocket?
i. Place all items on the belt, please.
j. You will be searched by someone from the security staff.

1	2	3	4	5	6	7	8	9	10
h									

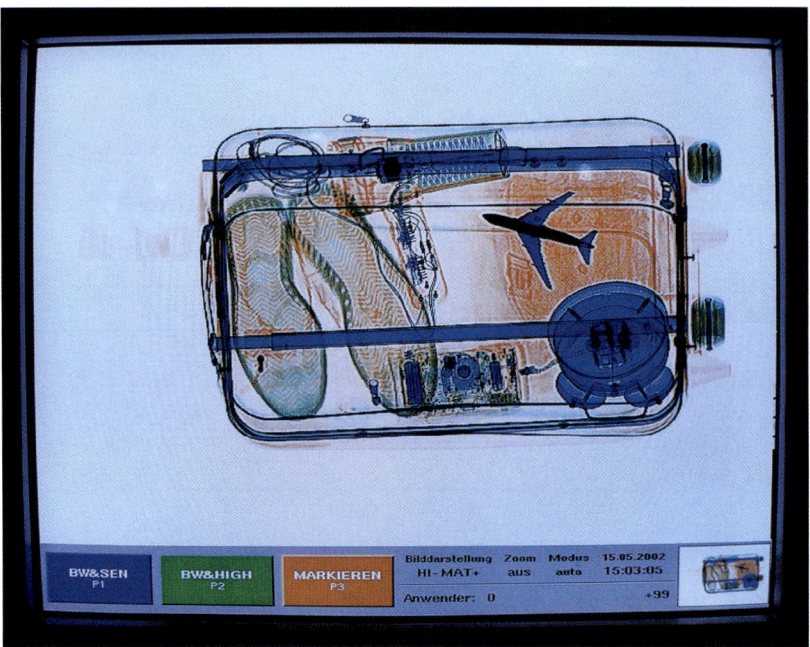

Task 6

In one of the airport's brochures you find the following information about security screening for passengers and their luggage.
Read the text. Then read the statements and write down whether they are true or false.

Before you reach the check-in desk, your check-in luggage will be screened. Your hand luggage will be screened later.

Please follow the signs to find the right entrance to the screening area.
Go to the screening area before going to the check-in desk. You will not
be checked in before your bags are screened.

If you wish to put items into or take items out of your check-in luggage, please do it before it is screened. After screening, the bags can no
longer be opened before being moved to the underground baggage sorting facility.

Place your check-in luggage on the conveyor belt of the screening devi-
ce. Before your luggage is returned to you, each item will be tagged. Do
not remove this tag. Untagged items of luggage are not accepted at the
check-in desk.

In the other terminal, your luggage will be screened in your absence in
the underground baggage sorting facility after you check in. You can
therefore go straight to the check-in desk.

In case your luggage has to be opened in your absence for a manual
check, you should not lock the bags that you check in. To secure your
bags it is advisable to use suitcase straps or cords.

underground	Untergrund
facility	Einrichtung
device	Gerät
to tag	etikettieren, mit einem Anhänger versehen
straight	direkt
manual	per Hand, manuell
strap	Riemen, Gurt
cord	Schnur, Band

	T	F
1. You have to tag your bag.		
2. Your hand luggage will not be screened here.		
3. Go first to the check-in desk before going to the screening area.		
4. Your luggage will always be screened in your absence.		
5. To secure your luggage you could use straps.		
6. You shouldn't lock the bags.		
7. You can only check in after your luggage has been screened.		
8. Your luggage might be checked manually.		
9. You can take items out of your luggage after having checked-in.		
10. You should secure your bag with a lock.		

92

A control centre - exploring articles and texts

In diesem Bereich lernen Sie, Informationen aus englisch-sprachigen Texten für den Bereich des Sicherheitsgewerbes zu entnehmen. Wichtig ist hierbei, sich gezielt Informationen zu beschaffen. Dies soll an verschiedenen Beispielen geübt werden.

Text 1 /part one

Tailoring our services to suit your needs.
Security services have a broad customer base covering every possible type of business and are committed to providing services which are both top quality and cost effective.
Because no two businesses are the same, they will develop a unique package of services designed specifically to meet your needs. Whether you need high profile or low key support, round the clock supervision or simply a keyholding service guarding will ensure you have all the protection you need:

Your security will be managed locally from one of our network of regional offices. Your safety and security specialist will have direct access to a 24 hour control centre at all times.
Assignment instructions following a full site survey are held as an indisputable record of the level of security we provide.

to tailor	anpassen
to suit	passen
to be committed to	verpflichtet sein
to provide	zur Verfügung stellen
cost effective	kostensparend
to develop	entwickeln
to design	entwerfen
of high profile	von hoher Qualität
low key support	Schließdienst
key holding service	Schlüsselverwaltung
to be managed	verwaltet werden
access	Zugang
assignment	Auftrag
indisputable	unstrittig

Assignments A to F

A. Read the general information. Then answer the following questions.

1. What do Security services offer to their customers?
2. What kind of service may the customer need?
3. From where will the customer's security be managed?
4. To what and when will have a security officer access?
5. What does the quality of the offered security guarantee?

1. ....
2. ....
3. ....
4. ....
5. ....

B. Match the words 1 to 9 with words in a-i which have the same meaning. The first one has already been done for you.

1. tailoring our services to suit
2. a broad customer base
3. cost effective
4. high profile support
5. low key support
6. keyholding service
7. direct access
8. assignment instructions
9. a full site survey

a. help of a fine level
b. easy to be reached
c. many customers
d. control by managing keys
e. make to fit
f. examine the whole place
g. worth the money spent on it
h. help by checking locks
i. information how to act

1 - e
2 -
3 -
4 -
5 -
6 -
7 -
8 -
9 -

C. Complete the parts in 1-6 with the parts given in a-f to form meaningful sentences.
    The first one has already been done for you.

1. Security services are committed
2. Services designed specifically
3. Guarding will ensure you have
4. Regional offices will manage
5. A control centre will have
6. The level of security is

a. protection for 24 hours.
b. direct access round the clock.
c. to come up to what is necessary.
d. of an unquestionable kind.
e. to providing services of high standards.
f. your security at the site.

1 - e
2 -
3 -
4 -
5 -
6 -

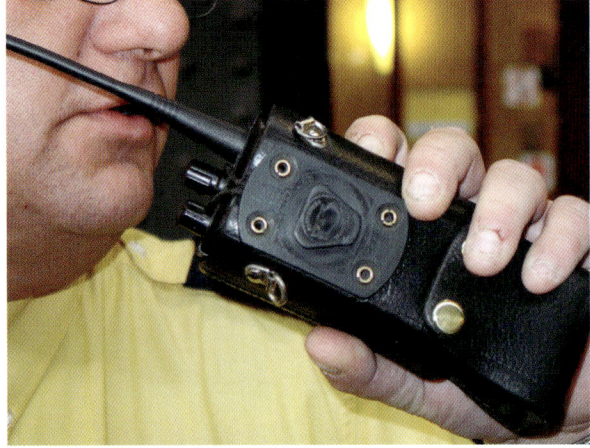

94

D. Complete the following text on the basis of the information given in the text. Fill in the blanks.

Security services have (1. viele Kunden)..
covering every possible (2. Branche)..The
services are both (3. Topqualität) ....
.... and (4. kostensparend) .... Whether you need
(5. 24 Stunden Bewachung)...
or simply a (6. Schließdienst) ....
Guarding will ensure the (7. Schutz) ....
..... you need. Your security comes from (8. Regionalbüros) ....
.... Your safety and security specialist will have (9. direkten
Kontakt) ....to a control centre (10. wann
auch immer) ....
(11. Auftragsanweisung) .... following a full
(12. Objektinspektion)..provide the
(13. Niveau) .... of security.

E. Write down whether the following statements are true or false.

1. Security services meet the needs of companies.
2. Services products are not listed in the introduction here.
3. Services range from low to high standards.
4. Access to control centres is not guaranteed outside peak hours.
5. Control centres take up a modest position in the services' system.
6. Assingment instructions are essential for the level of security.

	T	F
1		
2		
3		
4		
5		
6		

95

F. Find synonyms in the text for the following words. The first one has already been done for you.

1.	adapting	1.	tailoring
2.	to satisfy	2.	....
3.	wide	3.	....
4.	supplying	4.	....
5.	saving	5.	....
6.	companies	6.	....
7.	to create	7.	....
8.	superb	8.	....
9.	particularly	9.	....
10.	help	10.	....
11.	to control	11.	....
12.	passage	12.	....
13.	task	13.	....
14.	examination	14.	....
15.	unquestionable	15.	....
16.	account	16.	....

Text 1 / part two

Assignment instructions

Read them carefully and often

They are vital to the success of your job. They are written with the aim of giving you all the information possible about your particular assignment and what you must do to guard it against theft, fire, flood and vandalism.

Read them carefully and often. Sign them to indicate that you have read and understood them.

They are only of value if they are kept up to date, so if for any reason a change of circumstances necessitates their amendment, let your visiting supervisor know the details.

When changes are made to the assignment instructions you must sign to confirm that you have read and understood them.

Never forget to make your routine calls to the control centre.

Intruders

If for any reason you suspect the presence of intruders on your assignment, **Don't try to tackle them on your own** – call the Police and phone the control centre. When the Police arrive, let them in and give them every assistance.

If, during the course of your patrol, you surprise a person on the premises, ask him on whose authority he is there. Although you are not in possession of any special powers of arrest, you may detain him until the Police arrive if he cannot give a satisfactory explanation of his presence and you suspect he is committing or has committed an arrestable offence.

Night visits

You will receive frequent visits from regional supervisors. They are not 'snoopers' trying to catch you out, but hand–picked officers chosen for their security know-ledge.

vital to	entscheidend
aim	Ziel
particular	speziell
theft	Diebstahl
to sign	unterschreiben
to keep up to date	auf dem neuesten Stand bleiben
amendment	Veränderung
to confirm	bestätigen
intruder	Eindringling
control centre	Leitstelle
to suspect	verdächtigen
to tackle	angreifen, zur Rede stellen
premises	Gebiet, Gelände
authority	Befugnis, Befehlsgewalt
to detain	festhalten
to commit	begehen
offence	Vergehen, Straftat
snooper	Schnüffler
to catch out	hereinlegen
hand-picked	sorgfältig ausgewählt

96

Do not open-up until you have seen their ID card. Ask for the codeword.
If customers' staff seek entry, ask for identification. If they have none, phone
the control centre. Make sure that they sign the Guard Report Book.

Assignments A to F

A. Read the general information. Then answer the following questions.

1. What make assignment instructions so important?
2. Why must you sign for them?
3. What to do when an intruder is caught out?
4. What to do when visitors show up?

1. ....
2. ....
3. ....
4. ....

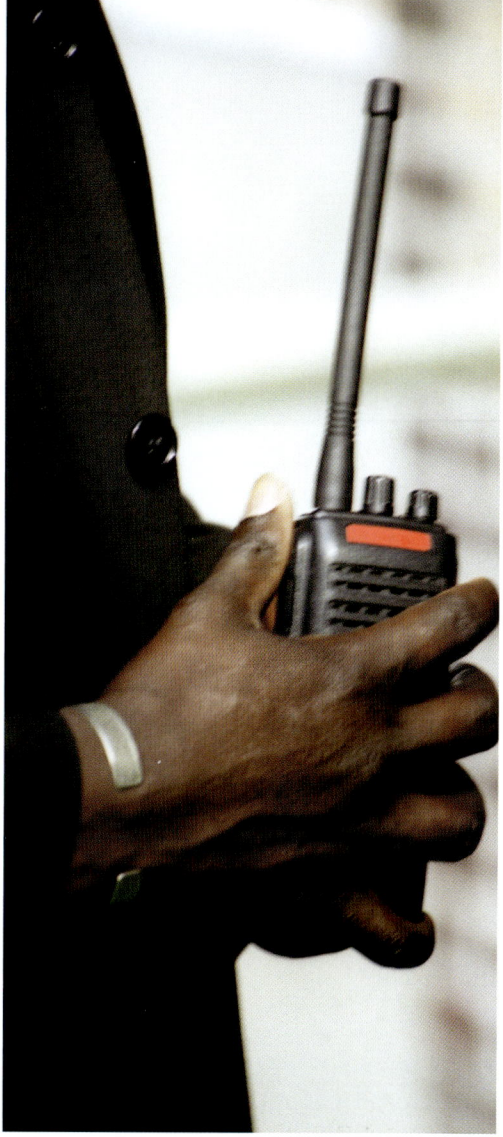

B. Match the words 1 to 13 with words in a-m which have the same meaning.
    the first one has already been done for you.

1. they are vital to	a. they are necessary for
2. with the aim of	b. they are of accurate information
3. your particular assignment	c. report at fixed times
4. guard it against	d. there are no doubts of his saying
5. they are kept up to date	e. on whose power or right
6. let your supervisor know	f. with the intention of
7. make routine calls	g. keep him waiting
8. on whose authority	h. your special task
9. you may detain him	i. show who you are
10. give a satisfactory explanation	j. inform your superior
11. he has committed an offence	k. protect it against
12. frequent visits	l. he has broken a law
13. an ID card	m. see each other often

1 - a
2 -
3 -
4 -
5 -
6 -
7 -
8 -
9 -
10 -
11 -
12 -
13 -

C. Complete the parts in 1-6 with the part given in a-f to form meaningful sentences.
The first one has already been done for you.

1. Instructions are important to be able to
2. You put down your signature
3. Let your superior know the details
4. If you suspect the presence of intruders
5. Though you cannot arrest a suspect
6. If staff seek entry

a. to show them that you have read and understood them.
b. you call the Police and phone the control centre.
c. you may detain him until the Police arrive.
d. when changes are made to the assignment instructions.
e. make sure they sign the Guard Report Book.
f. guard against theft, fire, flood and vandalism.

1 - f
2 -
3 -
4 -
5 -
6 -

D. Complete the following text on the basis of the information given in the text. Fill in the blanks.

They are written with (1. dem Ziel)...of giving you information about your (2. spezielle Aufgabe)............................ .... sign them to (3. wissen lassen) ....that you have read them. A change of (4. Umstände) .... necessitates their (5. Anpassung) .... If you suspect the (6. Anwesenheit) ....of (7. Eindringlinge) ...., don't try to (8. festnehmen) ....them (9. allein) .... Although you have not any special (10. Autorität jmd. festzunehmen) ...., you may (11. festhalten) .... him if he cannot give a (12. zufriedenstellend) .... explanation of his presence. You suspect

he has (13. verüben) .... an arrestable (14. Vergehen)
.... Supervisors are (15. sorgfältig ausgewählt)
.... officers chosen for their security
(16. Kenntnis) .... Do not open-up until you have seen their
(17. Personalausweis) ....

E. Write down whether the following statements are true or false.

	T	F
1. Assignment instructions tell you how to act in cases of emergencies.		
2. It is not important to keep instructions accurate.		
3. Intruders should be tackled by safety and security specialists only.		
4. Supervisors are too much interested in the affairs of guarding officers.		
5. Customers' staff must show their ID cards too.		
6. Customers need not sign the Guard Report Book.		

F. Find synonyms in the text for the following words. The first one has already
    been done for you.

1. necessary for   1. vital
2. goal   2. ....
3. protect   3. ....
4. stealing   4. ....
5. outburst of water   5. ....
6. smashing things up   6. ....
7. make known   7. ....
8. worth   8. ....
9. accurate   9. ....
10. improvement   10. ....
11. authority   11. ....
12. written statement   12. ....
13. prove   13. ....
14. regular   14. ....
15. trespasser   15. ....
16. buildings and ground   16. ....
17. owning   17. ....
18. keep back   18. ....
19. often   19. ....
20. come and see unexpectedly   20. ....

Text 2 / part one

First response

With years of experience and professionalism behind them the security industries
in the U.K. (United Kingdom) have a nationwide network of offices backed by a
highly advanced (NACOSS* approved) alarm monitoring and response centre, capable of handling up to one million alarm connections. Because of these extensive
facilities security services can meet all of your needs for:

response	Reaktion
experience	Erfahrung
backed by	unterstützt durch
highly advanced	fortgeschritten
to monitor	überwachen

*   Alarm monitoring
*   Remote CCTV (Closed Circuit Television) monitoring

The best warning system in the world is useless if you cannot react in time. Even
the best modern alarms can only warn of a problem. How big the problem becomes
may be up to you – you certainly don't want to let it slip out of control!

*NACOSS bedeutet National Approval Council for Security Systems

extensive	umfangreich
facilitiy	Einrichtung
remote	fern
resistance	Widerstand
interference	Störung
to direct	leiten
focussing on	richten auf
to track	verfolgen
would-be	potentiell

Alarm monitoring

If your alarm is networked to our Alarm Response Centre, you know you are in safe hands. Our industry approved alarm centre has been specially constructed to ensure its own resistance to interference or even attack. In fact, it is securely below ground against just about every eventuality.

Located in London, the centre handles alarm signals from all over the UK and is capable of directing specific action, immediately, anywhere in the country.

Remote CCTV monitoring

Our Alarm Response Centre can even direct CCTV cameras on specific sites. Cameras linked to our sophisticated system can be directed by an operator located hundreds of miles away from your site, focussing on and tracking any would-be intruder.

Assignments A to F

A. Read the general information. Then answer the following questions.

1. By what is the nationwide network of offices backed up?
2. What needs are met by the Alarm Response Centre?
3. How is the ARC built and where is it located?
4. What do CCTV cameras do?

1. ....
2. ....
3. ....
4. ....

B.   Match the words 1 to 13 with words in a-m which have the same meaning.
     The first one has already been done for you.

1.	first response	a.	contacts all over the country
2.	years of professionalism	b.	transmission of TV images along wires
3.	a nationwide network	c.	far reaching and helpful equipment
4.	a highly advanced centre	d.	prevent from obstruction
5.	alarm monitoring	e.	direct reaction
6.	remote monitoring	f.	anyone trying to trespass
7.	extensive facilities	g.	picking up alarm signals
8.	closed-circuit television	h.	managed by an expert
9.	specially constructed	i.	a lot of expertise
10.	resistance to interfere	j.	built for the purpose of
11.	sophisticated system	k.	detecting signals from a distance
12.	directed by an operator	l.	a highly advanced system
13.	any would-be intruder	m.	a site with the latest improvements

1 - e
2 -
3 -
4 -
5 -
6 -
7 -
8 -
9 -
10 -
11 -
12 -
13 -

C.   Complete the parts in 1-5 with the parts given in a-f to form meaningful
     sentences. The first one has already been done for you.

1.	The security industries have a nationwide network of offices	a.	alarm signals from all the UK.
2.	These extensive facilities can meet	b.	all of your needs for alarm monitoring and remote CCTV monitoring.
3.	Our alarm centre has been specially constructed	c.	focussing on and tracking any would-be intruder.
4.	Located in London, the centre handles	d.	capable of handling up to one million alarm connections.
5.	Cameras linked to our sophisticated system can be	e.	to ensure its own resistance to interference.

1 - d
2 -
3 -
4 -
5 -

D. Complete the following text on the basis of the information given in the text. Fill in the blanks.

With years of (1. Erfahrung)...and professiona-lism behind them the (2. Sicherheitsdienstleister) ....
are (3. in der Lage sein) .... of handling up to one million of (4. Alarmverbindungen) ....Because of these extensive (5. Einrichtungen) .... they can meet all your needs for (6. Alarmverfolgung) ....and remote (7. Kameraüber-wachung)..How big the problem becomes (8. könnte von Ihnen abhängen).. You don't want to let it (9. Kontrolle verlieren)..Our alarm centre has been specially (10. gebaut werden)................................to ensure its own (11. Widerstand)...................................to (12. Störungen) ....or even attack. Our Alarm Response Centre can (13. leiten)..................................CCTV cameras on (14. spezielle) ....sites.

E. Write down if the following statements are true or false.

	T	F
1. The security industries are represented in the whole UK.		
2. The response centre is known by the NACOSS.		
3. The ARC is found on tophill just outside London.		
4. Alarm signals from all over the UK are handled by the centre.		
5. CCTV cameras can be operated from far away.		
6. Our sophisticated system only works successfully in London itself.		

1. The security industries are represented in the whole UK.
2. The response centre is known by the NACOSS.
3. The ARC is found on tophill just outside London.
4. Alarm signals from all over the UK are handled by the centre.
5. CCTV cameras can be operated from far away.
6. Our sophisticated system only works successfully in London itself.

F. Find synonyms in the text for the following words. The first one has already been done for you.

1. reaction	1. response
2. expertise	2. ....
3. security companies	3. ....
4. contacts	4. ....
5. highly advanced	5. ....
6. monitoring	6. ....
7. signals	7. ....
8. aids	8. ....
9. distant	9. ....
10. guarantee	10. ....
11. force against	11. ....

102

12. obstruction   12. ....
13. safely   13. ....
14. GB   14. ....
15. concentrating on 15. ....
16. following   16. ....

Text 2/ part two

Technology as well as experience

Continuing investment in sophisticated communications technology has helped to distinguish the security industries. They realise that the demands of a multi-layered, national alarm and response service are extremely complicated. In this complex environment they have to know where all their vehicles and people are, day and night. They also need to know what they are doing and they need to be able to communicate with them at all times. It's the only way they can efficiently direct them to deal with problems. It is the only way they can provide their customers with the standard of service they expect. First response innovations include the phased introduction of real-time reporting and vehicle tracking equipment. This allows them to identify the position, direction and status of each patrol vehicle every 108 seconds. They also operate a high level command and control system which communicates to a hand held PC in every vehicle and which ensures the most efficient use of resources in an emergency or an alarm activation.

Control room duties

A control room is a facility for providing assistance and advice for guarding, mobile patrol and mobile supervisory staff in routine and emergency situations.

continuing	ständig
investment	Investition
sophisticated	hoch entwickelt
to distinguish	unterscheiden
demand	Forderung
multi-layered	vielschichtig
standard	Niveau
innovation	Innovation
phased	in Phasen
equipment	Ausrüstung
resource	Mittel
controller	Fachkraft für Notrufserviceleitstelle
observance of	Beobachtung von
appropriate	geeignet
to maintain	führen
restricted	beschränkt

The functions and duties of a controller therefore would be to provide for the following:

- Effective monitoring of guards, patrolmen and mobile supervisory staff by strict observance of routine telephone, radio or other communication procedures.

- Recording of all appropriate routine and emergency matters to enable management to deal quickly and efficiently with the company's contractual responsibilities.

- Maintaining a register of all keys held in the facility.

- Keeping and recording of the movement of client's keys in connection with a key holding or mobile patrol service.

Instruction for facility staff would include the following:
- Detailed explanation of duties
- Radio and telephone procedures
- Emergency procedures
- Location of and use of records.

Records of all incidents reported would contain as a minimum the following details:
- Date, time and place of the accident
- Date and time of reporting and by whom it was reported
- Nature of the accident
- Action taken, including onward reporting
- Action to be taken
- Names and addresses of all relevant persons present.

The facility shall be a restricted area open only to those authorised to enter.

Assignments A to F

A. Read the general information. Then answer the following questions.

1. What has helped to distinguish the security industries?
2. Why need they to communicate at all times?
3. What do first response innovations include?
4. What kind of facility is a control room in general?
5. What staff have access to a control room?

1. ....
2. ....
3. ....
4. ....
5. ....

B. Match the words 1 to 13 with words in a-m which have the same meaning. The first one has already been done for you.

1. continuing investments	a. putting money in regularly
2. multi-layered	b. speeding up on alarm reaction
3. complex environment	c. turn to for support
4. the phased introduction	d. register facts
5. use of resources	e. persons involved

6. used an alarm activation	f. split up in many divisions
7. supervisory staff	g. the following up on an account
8. observance of procedures	h. keeping a list
9. recording matters	i. complicated circumstances
10. maintaining a register	j. taking place by steps
11. onward reporting	k. a site within limits
12. relevant persons present	l. pay attention to rules
13. a restricted area	m. superiors

1 - a   8 -
2 -   9 -
3 -   10 -
4 -   11 -
5 -   12 -
6 -   13 -
7 -

C. Complete the parts in 1-6 with the parts given in a-f to form meaningful sentences. The first one has already been done for you.

1. The demands of a national alarm and response service
2. It's the only way they can
3. They operate a high level command and control system
4. The duties of a controller therefore would be to provide for
5. Instruction for facility staff would include
6. Records of all incidents reported would

a. which communicates to a hand held PC in every vehicle.
b. action taken, including onward reporting.
c. efficiently direct them to deal with problems.
d. recording of all appropriate routine and emergency matters.
e. are extremely complicated.
f. radio and telephone.

1 - e   4 -
2 -   5 -
3 -   6 -

D. Complete the following text on the basis of the informatin given in the text. Fill in the blanks.

Investment in (1. Kommunikationstechniken)..
has helped to (2. unterscheiden).. die
(3. Sicherheitsdienstleister) .... In this complex
(4. Umgebung) ....they have to know where all
their (5. Fahrzeuge)........... ....and people are, day and
night. It is the only way they can (6. zur Verfügung stellen).......................
..............their customers with the (7. Niveau).....................................
..........................of service they (8. erwarten) .... First
response (9. Innovationen) ....include the
(10. in Phasen stattfindend) ....introduction of (11. in
Echtzeit) .... reporting and vehicle (12. verfolgen)
.... equipment. A control room is a
(13. Einrichtung).................................... for providing (14. Unterstützung)
.... and advice in routine and (15. Notfällen)
.... The duties of a (16. Fachkraft für

Notrufserviceleitstellen)... therefore would be to provide for effective (17. Bildüberwachung)...
.... by strict (18. Beobachtung)... of (19. Kommunikationsvorgänge) ....

E.   Write down whether the following statements are true or false.

	T	F
1. A national alarm and respone service can efficiently deal with problems.		
2. First response innovations make it possible to identify each patrol vehicle every 108 seconds.		
3. Maintaining a register of all keys held is a controller's duty.		
4. Facility staff should be instructed on radio and telephone procedures.		
5. Records of incidents reported only contain the nature and place of the accident.		
6. A control room is an area open to all personnel.		

F.   Find synonyms in the text for the following words. The first one has already been done for you.

1. skill by doing   1. experience
2. putting money in   2. ....
3. with the latest improvements   3. ....
4. make different   4. ....
5. requirements   5. ....
6. difficult to do   6. ....
7. handle   7. ....
8. test for quality   8. ....
9. new things   9. ....
10. tools and things   10. ....
11. importance   11. ....
12. supplies   12. ....
13. serious situation   13. ....
14. accelerate reaction   14. ....
15. moving   15. ....
16. pay attention to   16. ....
17. order of doing things   17. ....
18. register   18. ....
19. control by managing keys   19. ....
20. joined with   20. ....
21. have limits   21. ....
22. right given to   22. ....

Direct Mail

Ein wichtiger Bestandteil der Arbeit im Sicherheitsgewerbe ist die Erstellung berufstypischer Standardschriftstücke, wie Brief, E-Mail und Fax. Im Folgenden soll nach einer Einführung zum formalen Aufbau das Aufsetzen eines Geschäftsbriefes in englischer Sprache geübt werden.

When you write a letter you should make sure that you:
•   Format your letter correctly.
•   Plan what you want the letter to say.

- Use a suitable tone. Make sure that the words you choose and the way you use them are suitable for the occasion.
- Use the best possible presentation for your letter and make sure that you check it.

to format	formatieren
to enquire	sich erkundigen
to stock	lagern
to purchase	käuflich erwerben
to look forward to	sich freuen auf

Format

Most formal letters follow the pattern used in the example below.

41 Rawlinson Road
Sutton Park
West Midlands
B98 5ZU

1. Your address
Notice how it is lined up
No punctuation is used

Shop Works
Customer Services Department
attn. Mr T. Bertram
Birmingham
B33 4KL

2. The name and address of the company and person you are writing to

17 July 2006

3. The date in full

Dear Mr Bertram,

4. The greeting
There is more about this

'Sunny Safety Glasses' sets

5. Heading
This makes it clear what the letter is about. But you do not have to use it

I am writing to enquire whether you are likely to stock any more 'Sunny Safety Glasses' sets, model number 09876 JX.

6. Introduction
Why you are writing

I bought several sets in your shop two years ago and would like to purchase new sets.
But I cannot find them for sale. I particularly wish to get this exact model as the team was very impressed with its appearance.

7. Body of the letter
Giving background information and explaining what you want in detail

If it is no longer produced, I should be most grateful if you let me know whether something similar is available and at what price.
Thank you very much for your help. And I look forward to hearing from you.

8. Conclusion
Saying what you like to happen

Yours sincerely,

9. Ending

C. T. Evans
Area Manager

Greetings and endings

It is important that the greeting and the ending of your letter tie up, as follows:

| to tie up | zusammenpassen |

- if you know the name of the persons you are writing to, use their name to greet them. For a formal letter you would usually use 'Dear' followed by 'Mrs/Ms/Miss/Mr', as appropriate, then the surname.
  Correct ending for this greeting: 'Yours sincerely'.
- if you do not know the name of the person you are writing to, you should greet them using 'Dear Sir or Madam'.
  Correct ending for this greeting: 'Yours faithfully'.

to wind up	abschließen
purpose	Absicht, Intention
slang	Umgangssprache
to assess	einordnen
letter of application	Bewerbungsschreiben
error	Fehler
sleeve	Hülle
tatty	schmuddelig
to reject	abweisen
decent	anständig
to smudge	verschmieren
to highlight	hervorheben

Plan

When you are preparing to write a letter, list all points you wish to include, then put them in a logical order. As you can see in the example, most letters include:

* **an introduction** explaining why you are writing
* the **body of the letter** giving background information and explaining what you want in detail
* a **conclusion** which 'winds up' the letter and makes it clear what its purpose is. If you wish the reader to **do** anything, make sure they know what you would like.

Tone

Make sure that the words you choose and the way you use them are suitable for the occasion. It is important that you make the best impression in your letter. In most formal letters:

* do not use slang or dialect phrases or words
* do not use short forms like you've or haven't
* do not write in a very personal way which may be inappropriate.

Presentation

Letters can be handwritten or word-processed. In an examination you have no choice, as your handwriting and presentation are being assessed. Likewise, some job advertisements ask you to handwrite a letter of application. However, if you have untidy handwriting, it might be worth word-processing an important letter.

* check your letter for spelling and punctuation errors. The final letter should be perfect.
* keep the letter neat and tidy, protect it in a plastic sleeve if necessary. Tatty letters will be rejected.
* write in the same colour ink throughout.
* use good quality paper and envelopes that match. This creates a good first impression.
* use a decent pen that does not smudge. Black is a good colour as it highlights the letters and makes them easier to read.

potentional	möglich
range	Angebot
options	Möglichkeiten
a number of	eine Anzahl
featured	abgebildet
to commision	berechnen
rates	Preise

Assignments A to D

Peter Pullover works for Flash Security. He runs the departments of Public Relations & Sales. P. R. has published the new catalogue offering a new set of security services' packages. Now Peter sends a direct mail letter to potential customers about the new catalogue.

Complete the following letter. Use a dictionary if necessary.

Dear Sir/ Madam,

It is our pleasure to inform you that Flash Security (1. fortführen mit).................................to extend its (2. Produktauswahl)...................... with the new catalogue. Several new options are (3. erwähnt)......................... ....; there are wider selections of (4. Lieferungen von)...................... ....security products.

For larger projects we can (5. anbieten)..................................... a number of (6. verschiedenen) ....contracts not (7. abgebildet)...... ....in this catalogue. To meet your special (8. Anforderungen).....................we can (9. entwerfen)................. ....and commission made to measure (10. Sicherheitspakete) ....The items featured in this range catalogue are those offered at highly (11. entwickelt)....................................levels and (12. kostenspa- rend) ....rates.

They are just a few of many security services products that we supply to our
(13. Kunden) ....with top service and
(14. Sachkenntnis)................................on the basis of value-for-money
prices.

If you are (15. interessiert).............................in more details, please
(16. anrufen) .... or fax our inquiries desk – 020 8722 2524 / 2530. You
can always (17. fragen) .... for an interview. (18. Wir freuen
uns darauf)...to doing business with you
(19. in naher Zukunft)..............................

Yours faithfully,

Peter Pullover
PR& Sales Manager

B.   Mail Deliveries had sent a copy of a special incident report to the local
     police station some time ago. Up to now it has not got the confirmation as
     is usual following procedures.

Tony Trunk, manager of M.D. and responsible for filing, is worried and asks Clare
Claddens, secretary of the department, to write a letter to Donald Duncan, chief
inspector of police.

Complete the following letter.

filing	Archivierung
file	Datei
attention (attn.)	Betreff (z. Hd.)
to owe	schuldig sein
a special incident	ein spezieller Vorfall
report	Bericht
an eyewitness	Augenzeuge
an account	ein Bericht

Flash Security Ltd
Sutton Park House
15 Park Road
Sutton
Surrey
SM1 4LD

Police Head Office
Attn. Chief Inspector Mr. Donald Duncan
29 Nobel Drive
Sutton Surrey
SM3 2KL

3 January 2006

Dear Mr Duncan,

When checking the (1. Dateien)...we found that
you owe us (2. eine schriftliche Bestätigung)...
...............................for the sending of (3. spezieller Bericht Nr. 36)...........
....dealing with (4. einem Verkehrsunfall auf
dem Gelände)...of one of our
customers, here in town.

Enclosed in the sending were an eyewitness account, a photocopy and (5. Skizze
der Situation) .... We are (6. überzeugt) ....
.... that there is a good (7. Grund) .... why we have
no (8. Reaktion)............................. within the (9. Zeitraum)....................
.... agreed on as you have always (10. gehandelt)
.... promptly so far.

109

Please see to it that (11. die Angelegenheit)...............................will be settled (12. so früh wie möglich)......................................Please disregard this reminder (13.wenn es bereits erledigt sein sollte)....................
....

Yours sincerely,

Tony Trunk
Manager Mail Deliveries

C.   Victoria Retreat is a place for old pensioners. It is an oasis of peace and quiet just outside a busy town. Flash Security has a contractual commitment here i. e. perform duties as effective guarding and survey customer key-holder details.

Recently there have been some disappointments about the quality of duties as carried out by guarding officers. The manager of the home is worried and decides to hand in a complaint at the head office at the attention of Mr Bert Belford. The date is 01 January 2006.
Complete the following letter.

commitment	Verpflichtung
i. e.	d. h.
to perform	erfüllen
to survey	überwachen
recently	kürzlich
on behalf of	im Namen von
due to	mit Dank an
to neglect	vernachlässigen
fire extinguisher	Feuerlöscher
unattended	unbewacht
at intervals	manchmal
to avoid	vermeiden
to urge	eindringlich bitten
annoyance	Ärger

Victoria Retreat
Owls House
34 Church Farm Lane
Sutton Park
Surrey
PO5 8RQ

Flash Security Ltd
1.   attn. (person's name)...........................
2.   (full address)....................................
....
....
....
....
3.   (date)............................

Dear Mr Belford,

It is on behalf of (4. Personal und Bewohner)...of the (5. Heim)... that I write to you.
Victoria Retreat is a (6. sicher).......................................place with a fine (7. Atmosphäre) ....It has a long standing reputation for that. This (8. zu verdanken) ....its inhabitants, staff and (9. nicht zuletzt)..your service men. So it is (10. mit Bedauern)...that we have to (11. mel-den)....................that recently there have been some (12. Enttäuschungen) ....about the (13. Qualität der Arbeit)..........
........................as carried out by guarding officers.

Instances of neglect of duties are:

* fire exits blocked or locked
* an empty (14. Feuerlöscher)... not reported on
* main entrance doors left (15. unbewacht)....................................at intervals
* broken (16. Scheibe)....................not reported on
* window fastenings not (17. kontrolliert)................................properly
* a (18. vermisst)...hose not reported on

We are (19. stolz).......................................of our environment and its reputation and we like to keep it that way. So I (20. dringend darum bitten)... you to (21. die Angelegenheit zu untersuchen)................................and we (22. erwarten) ....you to take (23. entsprechende).................... ....action to avoid further annoyance in the future. I (24. freue mich darauf)... to hearing from you soon.

Yours sincerely,

Leo Leftover
Manager Victoria Retreat

D. It is not only letters of this nature that come in, but fortunately there is news like this, too.

Andrew Mc Ginley is a safety and security specialist at the Safeway store in town, which is currently undergoing extensive renovation to become a hypermarket.

Complete this letter.

Dear Mr. Belford,

currently	gerade
persistent	beharrlich
targeting	zum Ziel haben
elusive	schwer zu fangen
hard evidence	klare Beweise
covert	versteckt
vigilance	Wachsamkeit
conduct	Vorgehen
tenacity	Hartnäckigkeit
thrilled	begeistert

Guarding officer Andrew Mc Ginley had just been (1. verantwortlich)....................................for arresting a persistent offender. This individual had been (2. zum Ziel haben)............................. the store over the past two years and was proving very elusive to arrest. It was (3. bekannt) ....that he was stealing goods from the store but (4. klare Beweise) ....was proving difficult. Andrew, by various means, kept this individual under close covert surveillance and was successful in (5. dem Ausführen von)........................... the arrest. Andrew is to be (6. beglückwünschen)...............................not only on his vigilance and professional (7. Vorgehen)...but also in his tenacity in making a good arrest. The store management were (8. begeistert)... with his performance. I felt I needed to write you to (9. feiern)....................................the kind of success and I believe Andrew to be an (10. hervorragend)..........................member of our service team.

Yours sincerely,

Alistair Rennie
Safeway Duty Manager

11//

At a sporting event - fire prevention

Wenn Sie als Schutz- und Sicherheitskraft in Unternehmen tätig sind, zählt zu Ihren Aufgaben auch das Beachten und die Überwachung objektbezogener Brandschutzbestimmungen.

Sie müssen sich mit der Funktion und Anwendung von Feuerlöschgeräten und technischen Anlagen auseinander setzen, das Gefährdungspotenzial abschätzen und bei sicherheitsbezogenen Schwachstellen entsprechende Verbesserungsvorschläge an die zuständigen Stellen (Feuerwehr, Werkschutz o. ä.) weiterleiten.

In Ihrer Ausbildung werden Sie aus diesem Grund u. a. mit den Grundsätzen der Brandbekämpfung und Eigensicherung bei Bränden vertraut gemacht. Sie lernen die verschiedenen Brandklassen zu unterscheiden und entsprechende Löscheinrichtungen auszuwählen.

Bei internationalen Veranstaltungen in Deutschland oder bei Einsätzen Ihres Unternehmens im Ausland kann es dabei zu Situationen kommen, in den Sie in englischer Sprache Anweisungen und Informationen geben müssen, um Menschen vor Gefahren zu warnen und aus Gefahrensituationen zu leiten.

Event

Security services provide top quality staff for a wide range of events, from sporting events to company conferences. The event market is split into three main sectors:

- Sporting and social events
- Exhibitions and venues
- Conferences.

Guarding has been trusted with high profile events for over decades, where the highest level of security is required to protect people and property. Expertise in high security events has led to consultative contracts overseas including training

venue	Tagung
exhibition	Ausstellung
expertise	Fachkenntnis
to gather	sammeln
regulations	Bestimmungen

113

and operational guidance. Whether the event is political or sporting, entertaining or informative, top secret or open to the public, guarding has the professional experience to provide the level of security required.

At the moment Stefan and Corinna from MB-security are working for a security team at the 23rd Ski Worldchampionships in France and will be appointed in various functions.
For the press conference taking place tomorrow in the St. George's Hotel Stefan wants to guarantee security. For that reason he gathers some information and wants to get to know the hotel regulations given to him by the operator.

Task 1

Track 54

Listen to the following conversation:

At the reception desk of the hotel Stefan and his French colleague he works with were given some information about the hotel's regulations for the press conference the following day. The conference room is on the second floor. Both Stefan and Jacques inspect the conditions on the spot.
In the folder he finds the German version of the emergency evacuation plan.

Task 2

Track 54

Listen to Task 1 again and mark the words which are used:

flame detector	fire detector
evacuation scheme	evacuation plan
fire doors	fire exit
exit graphics	exit signs
waste	rubbish
fighting equipment	fighting facilities
obstruction	obstacle
national standards	national requirements
pieces	devices
stairway	stairs

on the spot	vor Ort
folder	Ordner
cram-full	überfüllt
evacuation plan	Rettungsplan
fire exit	Notausgang
fire brigade	Feuerwehr
fire-fighting facilities	Löscheinrichtungen
to comply with	entsprechen, etw. erfüllen
fire prevention training	Brandschutzlehrgang
obstruction	Hindernis
national standards	nationale Anforderungen
storage	Lagerung
stairway	Treppe, Treppenhaus
to panic	in Panik geraten
fire detector	Brandmelder
flame detector	Brandmelder
evacuation scheme	Rettungsplan
fire doors	Brandschutztüren
exit graphic	Rettungsschild
waste	Abfall
fire-fighting equipment	Löscheinrichtungen
obstacle	Hindernis
national requirements	nationale Anforderungen
stairs	Treppe, Treppen

Task 3

Listen again to Task 1. How to say in English?

Track 54

1. Wo ist der Brandmelder?...
2. Alles muss schnell gehen...
3. Es wird überfüllt sein..
4. Hast Du kein Brandschutztraining gehabt?..
5. Kontrolliere, wo die Notausgänge sind..

Task 4

Check whether the following statements are true or false.

	T	F
1. There is a meeting in the hotel that day.		
2. Stefan has a look at the evacuation plan.		
3. The safety standard is guaranteed by the hotel manager.		
4. The hotel manager checks regularly the fire extinguishers.		
5. Jacques didn't follow a fire prevention training.		
6. Stefan always checks the storage.		
7. Stefan checks whether the exit doors are not locked.		
8. The exit signs should be visible.		
9. In the event of a fire most people panic.		
10. As a safety and security specialist you should be prepared for emergency.		

Task 5

Look at the evacuation plan and then study the conversation.

FLUCHT- UND RETTUNGSPLAN

to commence	beginnen
to recommend	empfehlen
path	Weg
to direct	anweisen
aisle	Gang
elevator	Fahrstuhl
to fight	bekämpfen
fire hose	Feuerlöschschlauch
calm	ruhig
to sound the alarm	Alarm schlagen
endangered	gefährdet
emergency phone	Notruftelefon
to equip	ausrüsten, ausstatten

Jacques

Stefan

Hi Stefan. The press conference will commence soon. Do you have a minute? I just have some more questions concerning the evacuation plan.

Sure. Do you have a question regarding the emergency exits?

Yes. Which one would you recommend?

Well, one should always choose the safest and shortest path. I suppose I would direct people to leave the floor via the stairways. There are two of them.

Standing here in the aisle at the orange coloured spot: Could I instruct the hotel residents: 'Follow the green fire exits signs, please!'?

Yes. And tell them: 'Don't take the elevator'. It could be dangerous. The arrow on the fire exit signs tells them where to go.

Would you start to fight the fire with one of the fire extinguishers or the fire hose?

Definitely not. What you learn in a fire prevention training is this: If there's a fire first stay calm, sound the alarm by the fire detector or if there's none call the fire brigade and your company's control centre. Then shout 'Fire' as you leave the building or try to rescue endangered persons. Close the doors and windows. But only if you can do so safely. Only if you're sure nobody's left in the building or you're safe start extinguishing the fire. In English the procedure is called RACE.

Standing here I would use the fire detector next to the window right there in that small room.

116

There's also an emergency phone here in that little room next to the lift.

Me, too.

Yes. I think this floor is very well equipped with fire protection features.

Well, thanks for the information.

Don't mention it.

RACE

Remove/**R**elocate individuals away from danger, if possible, without endangering your safety.

Activate Alarm: Pull fire alarm at pull-box, and/or call 112.

Confine/**C**ontain fire and smoke by closing doors and windows.

Extinguish/**E**vacuate

Task 6

Match the English and German words. The first one has already been done for you.

1.	commence	a.	ausgestattet
2.	hotel resident	b.	retten
3.	elevator	c.	empfehlen
4.	rescue	d.	Weg
5.	fire brigade	e.	beginnen
6.	calm	f.	ruhig
7.	path	g.	Feuerwehr
8.	endanger	h.	gefährden
9.	equipped	i.	Hotelbewohner
10.	recommend	j.	Fahrstuhl

117

```
1 - e          6 -
2 -            7 -
3 -            8 -
4 -            9 -
5 -           10 -
```

Task 7

Study the conversation in Task 5 again. Then work out this dialogue.

Thomas   Louis

Begrüßen Sie Ihren Kollegen.

                                              Grüßen Sie zurück.

Sagen Sie, dass Sie gerne
Informationen zum Fluchtwegplan
hätten. Sie haben keinen vom
Hotel erhalten.

                                              Fragen Sie, ob er Fragen zu den
                                              Brandschutzeinrichtungen hat.

Bestätigen Sie dies.

                                              Fragen Sie, was er wissen möchte.

Fragen Sie, wie viele Feuerlöscher
es auf jeder Etage gibt.

                                              Sagen Sie, dass es 4 Feuerlöscher auf
                                              jeder Etage gibt. Nur im Erdgeschoss gibt
                                              es mehr.

Fragen Sie, wie viele Fluchtwege es
auf den Etagen gibt.

                                              Sagen Sie, dass es zwei Treppenhäuser
                                              gibt.

Bedanken Sie sich.

                                              Sagen Sie, dass es nicht der Rede
                                              wert ist.

118

Task 8

How to say in English? Match the appropriate sentences.

1. Im Fall eines Feuers muss alles schnell gehen.
2. Keine Panik!
3. Bleiben Sie ruhig!
4. Notausgänge dürfen nicht verschlossen sein.
5. Wissen Sie, welcher Feuerlöschertyp verwendet werden muss?
6. Verlassen Sie das Hotel über das Treppenhaus.
7. Rennen Sie den Gang hinunter.
8. Im Fall eines Feuers benutzen Sie niemals den Fahrstuhl.
9. Überprüfen Sie, ob die Notausgänge frei zugänglich sind.
10. Haben Sie immer einen Feuerlöscher griffbereit.

a. Run down the aisle!   1. -
b. Do you know what kind of fire extinguisher to use? 2. -
c. Stay calm!   3. -
d. Always keep a fire extinguisher ready to hand.   4. -
e. In the event of a fire never use the elevator!   5. -
f. Emergency exits must not be locked.   6. -
g. Check if emergency exits are freely accessible.   7. -
h. In case of fire everything must go quickly.   8. -
i. Leave the hotel by the stairs!   9. -
j. Don't panic!   10. -

Conduct in case of fire.
1. Alarming
2. Rescuing
3. Extinguishing

Task 9

The Ski-Worldchampionships have already started and Corinna is on duty at the access control to the sporting events premises. A man is about to park his car close to the back entrance of the hotel.
Listen to the conversation.

FEUERWEHR
EINFAHRT

TAG UND NACHT
FREIHALTEN

Track 55

village	Dorf
to interfere	behindern
assembly area	Sammelstelle
to keep clear	frei halten
to get s.b. wrong	jmd. falsch verstehen
shuttle bus	Pendelbus
to file a complaint	Beschwerde einreichen
to ban	verweisen
to defy	hinwegsetzen
domiciliary right	Hausrecht
permit	Genehmigung
Wait and see!	Nur abwarten!

Task 10

Listen to the conversation of task 9 again. How to say in English?

1. Warten Sie ab!...
2. Ich werde eine Beschwerde gegen Sie einreichen.....................................
3. Es wird nicht lange dauern. ....
4. Ich bin Vorstand des Verbandes. ....
5. Sie brauchen nur 3 Minuten. ....
6. Sie widersetzen sich dem Hausrecht...
7. Im Falle eines Feuers ist dies die Sammelstelle. ....
8. Ich bin befugt, Besucher des Geländes zu verweisen. ....
9. Dieses Tor ist ein Rettungsweg...
10. Sie dürfen die Löscharbeiten nicht behindern. ....

Track 55

119

Task 11

Track 55

Now listen to the conversation again and check whether you used the right expressions.

Task 12

Study the conversation of Task 9 and 10 again. Then work out this dialogue.

Do you have a light?	Haben Sie Feuer?
smoking area	Raucherzone
to exercise	ausüben

Visitor   Safety and security specialist

Excuse me, Madam. Do you have a light, please?

Sagen Sie, dass das Rauchen im Konferenzraum verboten ist.

Well, I can't see any signs!

Weisen Sie auf das Schild am Eingang hin.

Is there any smoking area in the hotel?

Sagen Sie, dass aus Brandschutzgründen im gesamten Hotel das Rauchen nicht erlaubt ist.

I suppose I have to go outside.

Es tut Ihnen leid, aber auf dem gesamten Hotelgelände ist Rauchen verboten.
Sie teilen dem Gast mit, wenn er rauchend gesehen wird, wird er des Geländes verwiesen.

Are you exercising domiciliary rights?

Bestätigen Sie dies. Sagen Sie, dass Sie selbst Raucher sind und es Ihnen wirklich leid tut.

120

Task 13

Study the conversation in Task 1, 5 and 9 again. Then work out this dialogue.
Today Stefan is working at the jump. A group of visitors is blocking one of the
emergency exits.

Stefan   Visitor

Bitten Sie die Gruppe höflich, den
Notausgang frei zu machen.

Sagen Sie, dass Sie kaum etwas sehen
können.

Teilen Sie der Gruppe mit, dass Sie
enger zusammenrücken müssen. Der
Gang ist jederzeit freizuhalten.

Sagen Sie, dass der Bereich überfüllt ist.

Weisen Sie die Besucher darauf hin,
dass Sie sie vom Gelände verweisen
können, wenn sie nicht den
Anweisungen folgen.

Task 14

Jacques borrows Stefan's material from the fire prevention training. There are
some chapters in English.
Read the information carefully.

HOW TO USE A FIRE EXTINGUISHER
It is easy to remember how to use a fire extinguisher if you remember
the acronym, "PASS."

Pull
Aim
Squeeze
Sweep

Pull the pin
This will allow you to discharge the extinguisher.

Aim at the base of the fire
**Hit the fuel... if you aim at the flames, the extinguishing agent
will pass right through and do no good.**

Squeeze the top handle
**This depresses a button that releases the pressurized
extinguishing agent.**

Sweep from side-to-side until the fire is completely out.
**Start using the extinguisher from a safe distance away and then
slowly move forward. Once the fire is out, keep an eye on the area
in case it re-ignites.**

handle	Griff
pin	Sicherungspin
to discharge	entladen
to aim	zielen
temptation	Versuchung
agent	Mittel
to squeeze	pressen, drücken
button	Knopf
to sweep	hier: bewegen
flame root	Flammenkern
solid	fest
by fits and starts	in Intervallen
liquid	flüssig
in one step	in einem Schritt

THE CORRECT
EXTINGUISHING TACTICS

The correct extinguishing tactics:

Extinguish with the wind!

Extinguish at the flame root from front
to back!

In case of a fire of solid substances,
extinguish by fits and starts!

In case of a liquid fire, extinguish the
fire low above the fire area in one step

Task 15

Write down whether the following statements are true or false.

	T	F
1. You have to aim the fire extinguisher at the flames.		
2. If a liquid substance is burning, extinguish the fire by pressing the handle continually.		
3. At first you have to press the handle.		
4. Extinguish against the wind!		
5. If a solid substance is burning, extinguish by squeezing the handle irregularly.		
6. Even after the fire is out the area may re-ignite.		
7. Use the extinguisher from a safe distance.		
8. While extinguishing you have to move the hose from left to right.		
9. The fire extinguisher only works if you don't touch the pin.		
10. If you want to extinguish a fire the extinguishing agent has to fly to the flame root.		

Task 16

to notify	melden
location	Ort
to injure	verletzen

IF THERE'S A FIRE

SOUND THE ALARM

If you discover or suspect a fire, sound the building
fire alarm.

If there is no alarm in the building,
Notify other occupants by knocking on doors and
shouting
"Fire"
as you leave the building.

LEAVE THE BUILDING

Try to rescue others ONLY if you can do so safely.
Move away from the building at least 50 feet away,
out of the way of the fire department.
Don't go back into the building until the fire department say it is safe to do so.

CALL THE FIRE DEPARTMENT 112

Stefan and Jacques are talking about fire prevention procedures again. Jacques realized that he's got to follow a fire prevention training back home after the Ski-Worldchampionships.

Listen to the conversation and look at the graphic.

Track 56

Task 17

Track 56

Listen to the conversation of task 16 again. Write down whether the following statements are true or false.

1. The European emergency number is 9-1-1.
2. You should hang up the phone after having passed the necessary details on the emergency.
3. You should call the control centre after having discovered a fire.
4. You have to tell the operator your address.
5. Stefan isn't feeling well today.
6. Tell the operator where the main entrance is.
7. You have to inform the operator whether people are injured.
8. If you don't know what's burning you shouldn't use a fire extinguisher.
9. Jacques is glad that Stefan knows so much about fire prevention.
10. You don't have to dial 112 if you activated the building fire alarm system.

T	F

123

FOR ANY EMERGENCY DIAL 112

Emergency Call Procedure:

In any emergency call, the following procedure must be carried out

I.   Dial 112, or other emergency number.

II. Provide operator with the following information:
- Your name and phone number;
- Your location: Building name, floor and room numbers;
- Nature of emergency (fire, medical, chemical spill, etc);
- Number of injured people if any, and nature of injuries if known;
- Nearest building entrance where emergency personnel should go.

III. Designate someone to meet emergency personnel outside of building.

IV. Stay on line until you are excused by emergency operator.

Attention: If you are a person with a need of assistance to evacuate, request immediate assistance, inform the emergency operator of your location (safe room) and go to that location.

Task 18

Find 16 expressions of fire prevention in the word square (across and down)

T	Z	O	S	C	P	A	L	S	M	O	F	O
G	U	L	A	L	A	R	M	T	M	P	I	N
U	F	P	F	V	N	A	C	D	L	I	R	T
F	I	R	E	F	I	G	H	T	E	R	E	P
Z	R	B	T	C	C	M	O	E	X	U	P	E
B	E	N	Y	D	E	T	E	C	T	O	R	L
J	G	O	R	R	D	N	M	Z	I	L	E	Z
E	V	A	C	U	A	T	I	O	N	P	V	M
S	M	O	K	I	N	G	T	O	G	B	E	S
C	S	H	U	I	G	M	M	A	U	L	N	A
A	T	H	O	S	E	L	M	I	I	O	T	U
P	B	V	M	M	R	X	O	E	S	Y	I	M
E	X	I	T	S	I	G	N	I	H	R	O	H
R	H	K	C	A	O	I	T	E	E	B	N	M
O	C	D	I	S	C	O	V	E	R	P	A	R

126

Annex: knowing about grammar

Persons involved

You yourself and your fellow students

Event

Read the instructions. They tell you about:

1. Die Gegenwart
2. Die Vergangenheit
3. Der Artikel
4. Die Pluralform
5. Die Possessivpronomen
6. Viel und wenig
7. Steigerungsformen
8. Pronomen
9. Modalverben
   - a Notwendigkeit / Zwang
   - b Erlaubnis / Einwilligung
   - c Möglichkeit
   - d Fähigkeit
10. Die unregelmäßigen Verben

Here you find information to help you to understand how words can change, how words are used and what words mean.
Then you can do the tasks. You fill in the blanks.

1 Die Gegenwart

To be und to have

To be (sein) und to have (haben) sind zwei wichtige Verben.
Sie müssen die Verben lernen, da Sie wie im Deutschen sehr häufig verwendet werden.

to be		**sein**		to have		**haben**	
I	am	ich	bin	I	have	ich	habe
you	are	du	bist	you	have	du	hast
he	is	er	ist	he	has	er	hat
she	is	sie	ist	she	has	sie	hat
it	is	es	ist	it	has	es	hat
we	are	wir	sind	we	have	wir	haben
you	are	ihr	seid	you	have	ihr	habt
they	are	sie	sind	they	have	sie	haben

Achtung! Die Deklination ist abhängig von dem verwendeten Nomen.
Z. B. John ist im Garten.
Wer ist im Garten? **John**!
Das Nomen in diesem Satz ist John. Um den Satz kürzer zu machen oder weil man schon so oft John gesagt hat, kann man auch ‚er' gebrauchen.

John ist im Garten. - **Er** ist im Garten.

Der Gebrauch des Verbs ist in beiden Fällen gleich, nämlich: ist.

Im Englischen gilt dies auch: Wenn das Nomen ersetzt werden kann durch he, she und it, dann ist die entsprechende Deklination zu verwenden.
z.B.: My father is here - He is here.

Kann man entsprechend im Plural das Nomen ersetzen durch they (sie), dann ist der Satz wie folgt abzuwandeln:
Jane and Thomas are here – They are here.

Peter My brother The customer	he is
Mother Jane The saleswoman	she is
The department store The warehaose The article	it is
Mother and father The customers The saleswomen	they are

Task 1

Choose the right form of **to be**. Watch the noun!

1. The safety and security specialist .... in the hall.
2. Harrods....... the largest department store in Britain.
3. Here ...... a map of the ground floor.
4. I............ a sales manager.
5. We .... a school.
6. What........ the office hours?
7. The shop........... open from nine to six.
8. Friday............ our late night.
9. Watching people .... important to protect goods.
10. A department store .... a shop where they sell all kinds of things.

Task 2

Choose the right form of **to have**.

1. He ....a beautiful car.
2. The factory ... .several halls.
3. They..........just checked the rooms.
4. We...............many buildings on this site.
5. He...........bought a present for his son.
6. The customers.................a lot of parcels.
7. They usually.............a sandwich for lunch.
8. We ....fire extinguishers in the hallway.
9. After football the men ....a shower.
10. The thief.........stolen some shoes.

Regelmäßige Verben

Sie haben jetzt zwei unregelmäßige Verben gelernt, und zwar: to be und to have.
Unregelmäßige Verben sind Wörter, die eine eigene Konjugation haben.
Für die Konjugation von regelmäßigen Verben gibt es eine einfache Regel.

Die Regeln für die regelmäßigen Verben lauten:

I.   Bei den Formen ‚he', ‚she' und ‚it' wird ein ‚s' an den Infinitiv angehängt. Bei den anderen Formen verändert sich nichts – sie haben dieselbe Form wie der Infinitiv.

I	work	ich	arbeite
you	work	du	arbeitest
he	works	er	arbeitet
she	works	sie	arbeitet
it	works	es	arbeitet
we	work	wir	arbeiten
you	work	ihr	arbeitet
they	work	sie	arbeiten

I	give	ich	gebe
you	give	du	gibst
he	gives	er	gibt
she	gives	sie	gibt
it	gives	es	gibt
we	give	wir	geben
you	give	ihr	gebt
they	give	sie	geben

Task 3

Conjugate:

einpacken = to wrap   zuhören = to listen

I	....	....
you	....	....
he	....	....
she	....	....
it	....	....

we	....		....
you	....		....
they	....		....

II. Wenn ein Verb auf **'y'** endet und es steht davor kein Vokal, dann ändert sich bei he, she und it das **'y'** in **'ies'**.
Wenn vor der Endung **'y'** doch ein Vokal steht, dann wird an das **'y'** ein **'s'** angehangen.

Zur Erinnerung: Vokale sind a, e, i, o, u.

to worry		to pay	
I	worry	I	pay
you	worry	you	pay
he	worr**ies**	he	pay**s**
she	worr**ies**	she	pay**s**
it	worr**ies**	it	pay**s**
we	worry	we	pay
you	worry	you	pay
they	worry	they	pay

Task 4

Conjugate the verbs:

bleiben = to stay		heiraten = to marry
I	....	....
you	....	....
he	....	....
she	....	....
it	....	....
we	....	....
you	....	....
they	....	....

III Bei Verben, die auf einem sis-Laut (s.S. 137) enden, fügt man an bei he, she und it kein zusätzliches **'s'** hinzu, sondern **'es'**. Diese Ausnahmen sind z. B. he kiss**es**, she wash**es** usw. (he kisss gibt es nicht!)

Task 5

Conjugate:

hissen = to hiss	eilen = to dash	mischen = to mix
I .... you .... he .... she .... it .... we .... you .... they...........	I .... you .... he .... she .... it .... we .... you .... they...........	I .... you .... he .... she .... it .... we .... you .... they...........

IV   Hier folgen noch zwei wichtige Verben : to do und to go. Bei der
      Konjugation dieser Verben wird bei he, she und it auch ein **'es'** hinter den
      Infinitiv gesetzt, z. B. he go**es,** she do**es.**

Task 6

Conjugate the verbs:

tun, machen = to do   gehen = to go

I   ....
you ....
he   ....
she ....
it   ....
we   ....
you ....
they...........   ....

2   Die Vergangenheit

Regelmäßige Verben

Wenn Sie ein Verb in die Vergangenheit setzen wollen, müssen Sie die regelmäßigen und unregelmäßigen Verben kennen.
Wir beginnen mit den regelmäßigen Verben. Im Englischen gebraucht man bei
regelmäßigen Verben den Infinitiv und setzt an das Ende **'ed'**, unabhängig von
der Person.

arbeiten = to work

ich	arbeitete	I	work**ed**
du	arbeitetest	you	work**ed**
er, sie, es	arbeitete	he, she, it	work**ed**
wir	arbeiteten	we	work**ed**
ihr	arbeitetet	you	work**ed**
sie	arbeiteten	they	work**ed**

Wenn das englische Verb mit einem nicht hörbaren 'e' endet, dann wird nur ein **'d'** angehängt.

empfangen = to receive   entscheiden = to decide

I	received	I	decided
you	received	you	decided
he, she, it	received	he, she, it	decided
we	received	we	decided
you	received	you	decided
they	received	they	decided

Task 7

Conjugate the verbs in the past tense:

sprechen = to talk	verdienen = to deserve	sehen = to look	vergleichen = to compare
I	....	....	....
you	....	....	....
he	....	....	....
she	....	....	....
it	....	....	....
we	....	....	....
you	....	....	....
they............	....	....	....

Task 8

Conjugate the verbs in the past tense:

verdienen = to earn	beobachten = to watch	vorbereiten = to prepare
I	....	....
you	....	....
he	....	....
she	....	....
it	....	....
we	....	....
you	....	....
they............	....	....

Wenn der Infinitiv auf **'y'** endet, und davor ein Konsonant steht, dann endet es in der Vergangenheitsform auf **'ied'**.

Gegenwartsform		Vergangenheitsform	
I	worry	I	worried
you	worry	you	worried
he	worries	he	worried
she	worries	she	worried
it	worries	it	worried
we	worry	we	worried
you	worry	you	worried
they	worry	they	worried

132

Wenn der Infinitiv auf **'y'** endet, und davor ein Vokal steht, dann endet das Verb in der Vergangenheitsform ganz normal auf **'ed'.**

Gegenwartsform		Vergangenheitsform	
I	stay	I	stay**ed**
you	stay	you	stay**ed**
he	stays	he	stay**ed**
she	stays	she	stay**ed**
it	stays	it	stay**ed**
we	stay	we	stay**ed**
you	stay	you	stay**ed**
they	stay	they	stay**ed**

Task 9

Conjugate the verbs in the past tense:

sich beeilen = to hurry   tragen = to carry

I	....	....
you	....	....
he	....	....
she	....	....
it	....	....
we	....	....
you	....	....
they	....	....

Task 10

Conjugate the verbs in the past tense:

trocknen = to dry	verneinen = to deny	begraben = to bury

I	....	....	....
you	....	....	....
he	....	....	....
she	....	....	....
it	....	....	....
we	....	....	....
you	....	....	....
they	....	....	....

Task 11

Insert the correct form in the past tense:

1. They..........................to clean the house. (to try)
2. He..........................the bathroom. (to clean)
3. He..........................to her.(to propose)
4. She........................to become his wife. (to agree)
5. They.......................each other. (to marry)
6. I...........................you a miracle. (to promise)
7. He ....for the job. (to apply)
8. She..........................on you. (to depend)

133

9. Jane........................an old bike. (to possess)
10. They........................a house. (to own)

Task 12

Insert the correct form in the past tense:

1. We ....him.(to believe)
2. He.............................gas. (to smell)
3. It..............................hot. (to taste)
4. They.........................music. (to compose)
5. He............................pretty dull.(to seem)
6. They.........................to paint the house.(to start)
7. James.......................the door.(to paint)
8. I...............................that absolutely.(to deny)
9. They.........................for freedom.(to cry)
10. Mum.........................a heavy bag.(to carry)

Unregelmäßige Verben

Es gibt für unregelmäßige Verben keine Regel, deshalb müssen Sie die unregelmäßigen Verben einfach auswendig lernen. Sie finden eine Liste der unregelmäßigen Verben im Anhang(seite 152 ff.). Die Vergangenheitsformen stehen in der
zweiten Reihe. Die erste Reihe führt die Infinitive auf, die dritte Reihe das
Partizip Perfekt.

3   Artikel

Artikel stehen vor Nomen.
Im Deutschen unterscheidet man:

die bestimmten Artikel: der, die, das
die unbestimmten Artikel: ein, eine, einen

Ich will einen roten Tisch.
Ich will den roten Tisch, der dort steht.
Er wohnt in einem alten Haus.
Das Haus an der andere Seite ist alt.

Der unbestimmte Artikel hat keinen Plural.

eine Kuh   Kühe

Im Englischen gibt es nur den bestimmen Artikel **the**

der Tisch   the table
das Haus   the house
der Stuhl   the chair
das Kind   the child
die Kuh   the cow

Aussprache:
Wenn man nach dem – **the –** einen Vokal hört, ist für the die Aussprache **thie.**
Hört man einen Konsonanten, dann ist für the die Aussprache **thuh.**

134

Der unbestimmte Artikel ein/eine wird im Englischen mit **a** oder **an** gebildet.

a: gebraucht man, wenn man einen Konsonanten hört
   a cow
   a man
   a university (sie hören ein 'j')
   a uniform (sie hören ein 'j')

an: gebraucht man, wenn man einen Vokal hört
    an apple
    an eye
    an hour (sie hören nämlich 'our')

Task 13

Insert the indefinite article:

1. ....   apple
2. ....   orange
3. ....   melon
4. ....   pineapple
5. ....   coconut
6. ....   onion
7. ....   pea
8. ....   avocado
9. ....   grapefruit
10 ....   tangerine
11 ....   pear
12 ....   banana
13 ....   cauliflower
14 ....   sprout

4   Der Plural

Ein Nomen können Sie erkennen, wenn Sie einen Artikel davor setzen können,
im Deutschen nämlich das, der, die, ein, eine.

Der Junge legt den Bleistift auf den Tisch.
Das Essen wird auf den Tisch gestellt.

Im Englischen gibt es verschiedene Möglichkeiten, einen Plural zu formen. Bitte
lernen Sie diese Möglichkeiten und Ausnahmen von den Regeln auswendig.

a.   Meistens endet die Pluralform des Nomens auf **'s'**:

   one bag   two bag**s**
   one table   two table**s**
   one house   two house**s**
   one chair   two chair**s**

b.   Wörter mit einen 'sissenden'-Laut, wie 's', 'ss', 'sh', 'x' und 'ch' enden auf ,**'es'**:

   one glass   two glass**es**
   one smash   two smash**es**
   one box   two box**es**
   one match   two match**es**

135

c. Wörter, die mit einem Konsonanten (b, d, k usw.) und **'y'** enden, enden im Plural auf ' **ies'**:

one ferry	two fer**ies**
one lady	two lad**ies**

Bei Wörtern, die auf einem Vokal (a,e,i,o und u) und **'y'** enden, enden im Plural mit **'s'**:

one toy	two toy**s**
one key	two key**s**

d. Nomen, die auf **'f'**, oder **'fe'** enden, besitzen im Plural die Endung **'ves'**:

one knife	two kni**ves**
one wife	two wi**ves**
one shelf	two shel**ves**
one half	two hal**ves**
one thief	two thie**ves**
one loaf	two loa**ves**

Ausnahmen:

one roof	two roof**s**
one safe	two safe**s**
one chief	two chief**s**

e. Bei der Endung eines Nomens auf **'o'**, endet die Pluralform auf **'es'**:

one tomato	two tomato**es**
one potato	two potato**es**

Bei Nomen mit der Endung **'o'**, die nicht aus der englischen Sprache kommen, hat die Pluralform ein **'s'**:

one kilo	two kilo**s**
one piano	two piano**s**
one photo	two photo**s**
one dynamo	two dynamo**s**

f. Ausnahmen von den Regeln sind folgende Nomen. Lernen Sie sie gut. Sie kommen häufig vor:

one woman	two women
one man	two men
one mouse	two mice
one louse	two lice
one child	two children
one tooth	two teeth
one foot	two feet
one goose	two geese

g. Im Plural nicht veränderbare Nomen sind:

one sheep	two sheep
one deer	two deer
one series	two series
one aircraft	two aircraft

136

In den folgenden Aufgaben kommen sowohl Singular- wie Pluralformen vor.
Lernen Sie daher erst die Pluralformen und sehen Sie dann, ob sie die Aufgaben
problemlos lösen können.

Task 14

Form the plural:

1. boy   ....
2. house   ....
3. knife   ....
4. sheet   ....
5. place   ....
6. box   ....
7. match   ....
8. potato   ....
9. photo   ....
10. chair   ....
11. mouse   ....
12. day   ....
13. child   ....
14. penny   ....
15. lady   ....
16. shelf   ....
17. pint   ....
18. woman   ....
19. bottle   ....
20. rose   ....
21. pot   ....
22. dynamo   ....
23. sheep   ....
24. tooth   ....

Task 15

Insert the correct form in the plural:

1. There were two ....(shelf) with toiletpaper.
2. They caught three................................(thief).
3. Two ....(kilo) of.....................(tomato), please.
4. They didn´t develop the ....(photo).
5. Ten..................(box) of......................(match), please.
6. He gave me two........................(pound) and forty pence.
7. The.....................(child) were playing with some ....(toy).
8. There are three.......................(ferry) from Holland to England.
9. Many........................(lady) were present at the fashion show.
10. She doesn´t like...............................(potato).

5 Possessivpronomen

Das Possessivpronomen benutzen wir, um zu zeigen, von wem was ist.

Das Haus von meinem Vater.
Das Fahrrad von meinem Bruder.
Der Garten von meinem Opa.

Es ist auch möglich, zu sagen:

Das Haus meines Vaters.
Das Fahrrad meines Bruders.
Der Garten meines Opas.

Im Englischen wird die Besitzform angegebenen mit einem **'s'** oder einer Konstruktion mit **'of'.**

Lernen Sie bitte die folgenden Sätze:

My father´s house
John´s book
The dog´s basket
The cat´s tail
A month´s salary
A week´s time
The legs of the table
The doors of the car
The windows of the shop

Aus diesen Sätzen geht hervor, dass:

*   **'s'**– benutzt wird bei Personen, Tieren und Zeit
*   **'of'**– benutzt wird bei Gegenständen.

Wenn Nomen auf **'s'** enden, dann setzt man in England nur ein Apostroph hinter das Wort.

My brother´s bike
Both my brothers´ bikes
Charles´ books
A two weeks´ holiday

Manchmal können Sie Folgendes lesen:

The butcher´s
My aunt´s

In England meint man damit:

The butcher's shop
My aunt's house

Task 16

Choose the right answer:

1. Who wants   a) newspapers of yesterday?
          b) yesterday´s newspapers?
2. I often rush into a a) McDonald´s to have a hamburger.
          b) McDonald to have a hamburger.
3. In films the   a) murderer of the victim is always caught.
          b) the victim´s murderer is always caught.
4. Who is   a) the author of the book?
          b) the book´s author?

5. The   a)   lid of the teapot was broken.

                  b)   teapot´s lid was broken.

6. She went to a   a)   girl´s school.

                  b)   girls´ school.

7. The   a)   office of the manager is cleaned once a week.

                  b)   manager´s office is cleaned once a week.

8. The   a)   cat´s basket is in the corner.

                  b)   basket of the cat is in the corner.

9. I have found   a)   James´coat.

                  b)   James´s coat.

10. The   a)   restaurant´s name is printed on the menu.

                  b)   name of the restaurant is printed on the menu.

6   Viel und wenig

‚Viel' oder ‚wenig' können Sie ins Englische unterschiedlich übersetzen.
Zuerst müssen Sie allerdings wissen, was zählbare und unzählbare Nomen sind.
Zählbare Nomen haben eine Pluralform:

| ein Becher | a cup |
| zwei Becher | two cups |

| ein Mann | one man |
| zwei Männer | two men |

Nicht-zählbare Nomen haben keinen Plural:

Liebe	love
Reis	rice
Milch	milk
Wissen	knowledge

‚Viel' und ‚wenig' haben unterschiedliche Übersetzungen:

much	viel	little	- wenig
many	viel	few	- wenig
a lot of	viel		

Much und **little** werden verwendet bei **nicht-zählbaren** Nomen.

much tea   little time

Many und **few** werden verwendet bei **zählbaren** Nomen.

| one sheep | two sheep | many sheep | few sheep |
| one carrot | two carrots | many carrots | few carrots |

Sie verwenden **many** und **few** auch bei Wörtern wie **police** and **people**.

A lot of wird sowohl bei zählbaren als auch unzählbaren Nomen verwendet:

| much money | a lot of money |
| many coins | a lot of coins |

139

In der Umgangsprache finden Sie häufiger die Anwendung von **a lot of** an Stelle von **much**.

Sie können auch *too much* sagen, aber die Verwendung von much oder many erfolgt eigentlich nur bei Fragensätzen oder verneinenden Sätzen.

Bei verneinenden Sätze wird immer **not** verwendet.

Do you drink much tea?	Yes, I drink a lot of tea.
Can I have a cup tea ?	I am afraid there isn´t much left.
Are there many boxes?	Yes, there are a lot of them.
Are there many boxes?	I am afraid there aren´t many of them.

Task 17

Insert the correct form:

much or many:

....	trouble
....	pupils
....	pictures
....	ribbons
....	geese

few or little:

....	press ups
....	ice
....	customers
....	people
....	boxes

Task 18

Insert **much** or **many** .

1. There isn´t ....time left.
2. I usually drink.............milk.
3. There aren´t..............men in here.
4. ....people go to Harrods.
5. ....tourists visit the 'KADEWE'.
6. Are there ....articles in the freezer?

Task 19

Insert **much** or **many** .

1. The staff was chosen with ....care.
2. We often pay.............money for these goods.
3. In summer we have ....sun.
4. Do you like.............sugar in your tea?
5. We didn´t see ....police.
6. He went to ....trouble to help you.
7. They spent...........time finding the fire.
8. There weren´t.............people here last Sunday.
9. We had too ....to do yesterday.
10. She gave ....guests a badge.

Task 20

Insert **a few** or **a little**.

1. Could you give me.................of these papers?
2. There was ....milk in the bottle.
3. I had to write ....people a letter.
4. There was only...............time to get the people out of the building.
5. What´s going on? It´s ....too quiet in here.
6. Bridget was ....minutes late this morning.
7. You spilled ....water on the floor.
8. There are still.......................cars in the park.
9. It´s ....late, don´t you think?
10. Here are ....men to help you.

7 Steigerungsformen

Im Englischen verwendet man die Steigerungsformen durch:

1 das Anhängen von **er, est** an das Adjektiv. Aber nur, wenn es nicht mehr als eine oder zwei Silben hat.
Achten Sie auf die Veränderungen in der Orthographie.

small	small**er**	small**est**
big	bigg**er**	bigg**est**
noisy	noisi**er**	noisi**est**
quiet	quiet**er**	quiet**est**
nice	nic**er**	nic**est**

2 Bei mehrsilbigen Wörtern verwendet man **more** und **most**.

comfortable	**more** comfortable	**most** comfortable
expensive	**more** expensive	**most** expensive
beautiful	**more** beautiful	**most** beautiful

3 Es gibt auch einzelne unregelmäßige Formen. Die Wichtigsten sind:

good	better	best
bad	worse	worst
modern	more modern	most modern
much/many	more	most
little (wenig)	less	least
little (klein)	smaller	smallest

Task 21

Choose the right form of the words in brackets.

1. It is much..........(easy).......to work at home than working on a UN mission.
2. She is ......(nervous)..........soldier of them all.
3. He is the......(polite).......officer I have ever met.
4. Private Miller has the ....(complete)....set of Englisch dictionaries of the platoon.
5. Eager Beaver is the ...(wild)....guard dog I know.

141

6. This is the ....(welcome)....news we have had for months.
7. Physical exercises will make you feel much....(fit).
8. This rifle is ....(heavy)....than I thought.
9. Roads in the USA are....(wide) than I expected.
10. This boat will take you to the ...(great)...places in the world.
11. This bread tastes....(good)....than this morning's.
12. Our company has....(modern).....equipment than we had in the nineties.
13. English cheeses taste....(bad)...than Dutch cheeses.
14. This forest is the ...(quiet)....place I know.
15. The ....(expensive)....car is that Rollce Royce.

8 Pronomen

Wenn Sie auf etwas hinweisen möchten, verwenden Sie Demonstrativpronomen.
Gängige Demonstrativpronomen sind im Englischen: **this, that, these** und **those**.

Singular	nahe	weit
	this	that

Plural	nahe	weit
	these	those

Task 22

Insert: **this, that, these** or **those**:

1. ....(diese) are nice shoes.
2. Where did you buy........(diese) boots?
3. In........(diesem)shop over there.
4. ....(diese) vase is nicer than ....(diese) one.
5. ....(dieser) old man is ninety years old.
6. ....(diese) books are too difficult.
7. ....(diese) books are more useful.
8. Who is ....(das) girl?
9. We were looking for...........(diese) diaries.
10. ....(diese) saucers don´t match ....(diesen) cups.

Fragen bei Personen:

Wenn sie Fragen stellen, die sich auf eine Person beziehen, verwenden Sie das
Fragepronomen **who.**

1.	Who took my car?	Wer hat mein Auto mitgenommen?
2.	Who are those boys?	Wer sind diese Jungs?
3.	Who is he?	Wer ist er?
4.	Who did you speak to?	Mit wem hast Du gesprochen?
5.	Who did he see?	Wen hat er gesehen?

Wenn Sie wissen wollen, von welcher Person etwas ist, dann verwendet man im
Englischen **whose.**

142

1. Whose books are these?   Von wem sind die Bücher?
2. Whose bike is that?   Wessen Fahrrad ist das?
3. Whose house is this?   Wessen Haus ist das?

Task 23

Insert **who** or **whose**:

1. .... took the money?
2. .... toys are these?
3. .... house is for sale?
4. .... did you give the change to?
5. .... did you tell the news to?
6. .... purse was stolen?
7. .... is that customer?
8. .... is branch manager?
9. .... money was stolen?
10. .... is there?

Fragen bei Sachen:

Möchten Sie eine Frage zu einer Sache stellen, dann müssen Sie **what** verwenden.

1. What did you see?   Was hast du gesehen?
2. What did you buy?   Was hast du gekauft?
3. What caused the accident? Was verursachte den Unfall?
4. What is she wearing?   Was trägt Sie?
5. What time is it?   Wie spät ist es?
6. What was the show like?   Wie war die Vorstellung?

Task 24

Translate these 5 lines:

1. Was hast du getan?
2. Was macht er?
3. Wie lautet seine Adresse?
4. Wie war das Wetter?
5. Wie sieht er aus?

Task 25

Insert **who** or **what**.

1. .... did he make?
2. .... has she bought?
3. .... did you see? Your sister?
4. At..........time do you close?
5. ....did you see? I saw the accident.

Wenn eine Entscheidung zwischen verschiedenen Möglichkeiten besteht, verwenden Sie bei Fragen **which.**

Hier besteht kein Unterschied zwischen Personen oder Sachen. In beiden Fällen wird **which** verwendet.

1. Which of the children is the eldest?
   Welches ist das älteste Kind?
2. Which school does she go to?
   Zu welcher Schule geht sie?
3. In which department does he work?
   In welcher Abteilung arbeitet er?
4. Which article would you like to see?
   Welche Artikel würden Sie gerne sehen?

Task 26

Insert **who, whose, which** or **what**:

1. .... of these articles do you prefer?
2. .... shoes do you like best?
3. .... size do you take?
4. .... CD would you like to hear?
5. .... watch is on the table?
6. On........................... floor can I find the restaurant?
7. .... did you give mother for her birthday.
8. .... is that man over there? It´s my uncle.
9. .... is this man doing over there? He is painting.
10. .... blouse are you wearing? It´s my sister´s.

Task 27

Insert **who, whose, which** or **what**:

1. .... bike is that?
2. .... are you looking for?
3. .... do you want?
4. .... of these dresses would you like to try on?
5. .... of the cd players is the easiest to operate?
6. .... did you phone, while I was out? My father.
7. .... is the price of this article?
8. .... car would you buy, if you had a lot of money?
9. In........................... month was he born?
10. .... did he win? A gold medal.

Weitere Fragepronomen sind:

1. When did you see him?   Wann hast du ihn gesehen?
2. When does the shop close?   Wann schließt das Geschäft?
3. When is late night shopping?   Wann ist der verkaufsoffene Abend?
4. Where is the entrance?   Wo ist der Eingang?
5. Where do I find socks?   Wo kann ich Socken finden?
6. Where are the toilets?   Wo sind die Toiletten?
7. Why did you do that?   Warum machtest du das?
8. Why did you give change?   Warum gabst du Wechselgeld?
9. Why did you leave?   Warum gingst du weg?
10. How did you do that?   Wie hast du das getan?

144

11. How do you use this?   Wie gebrauchst du dies?
12. How wide is the case?   Wie breit ist die Kiste?

Ferner müssen Sie die folgende Ausdrücke lernen:

1. How much did you pay?   Wie viel hast du bezahlt?
2. How much is it?   Wie viel kostet es?
3. How much do I owe you?   Wie viel schulde ich dir?
4. How many books?   Wie viele Bücher?
5. How many tables?   Wie viele Tische?
6. How many euros?   Wie viele Euros?

How many wird gebraucht, wenn ein Nomen folgt, das zählbar ist, sonst
verwendet man **how much**.

Task 28

Insert **who, whose, what, which, when,where, why, how, how much** or **how
many**:

1. .... did you see that black coat? On the market.
2. .... colours did they have? They had all colours.
3. .... did you see it? I saw it yesterday.
4. .... was it? It only cost 20 euros.
5. .... didn´t you buy it? I didn´t have enough money.
6. .... is your butcher? Mr. Mulligan is my butcher.
7. .... is his shop? It is just down the road.
8. .... is it open? Only in the mornings.
9. .... is it closed in the afternoon? Because his wife is in hospital.
10. .... days a week is it open? Six days.

Task 29

Insert **who, whose, what, which, when, where, why, how, how much** or **how
many**:

1. .... necklace is this on the table? It is Mum´s.
2. .... is it on the table? She was showing it to Dad.
3. .... is Mum now? She has gone to the neighbour´s.
4. .... neighbour, we´ve got four of them? Mrs. Kinnock.
5. .... did she go there? She has gone for some sugar.
6. .... do you refill the shelves? On Monday.
7. .... not before? Because, Mr. Marks is on holiday.
8. .... has he gone to? I believe to Greece.
9. .... long has he been there? Two weeks.
10. .... did he go there? He went by plane.
11. .... are my trousers? At the dry cleaner´s.
12. .... did you take them there? They were dirty.
13. .... will they be back? Next week I think.
14. .... not before the weekend? He is closed on Friday.
15. .... will it cost? 8 euros I think.

9 Modale Hilfsverben

Die Hilfsverben, die nun besprochen werden, werden auch Modalverben genannt. Sie geben nicht eine spezielle Zeit an, aber:

Notwendigkeit / Zwang	müssen	must, have to, should
Erlaubnis / Einwilligung	mögen, können	may, can, could
Möglichkeit	mögen, können	may, might, can, could
Fähigkeit	können	can, could

Es gibt noch eine Besonderheit bei den Modalverben: die meisten können Sie gewöhnlich nur in der Gegenwart verwenden.
Bei Verwendung der Vergangenheit oder einer anderen Zeit, muss ein anderes Modalverb gewählt werden.

a Notwendigkeit/ Zwang

I **have** to be home at 8 o´clock.
I **must be** home at 8 o´clock.

'Müssen' wird ins Englische mit **to have** oder **must** übersetzt. Manchmal ist es nicht von Bedeutung, welche Form man gebraucht. Es gibt aber Situationen, wo man nur die eine oder andere Form gebrauchen kann.

Must wird grundsätzlich verwendet, wenn eine persönliche Meinung ausgedrückt werden soll.

I don´t like your perfume. You **must** change it.
I **must** go now, I have a lot of work to do.
Children, you **must** be quiet now.

To have to verwenden Sie, wenn es eine Tatsache, keine persönliche Meinung ist.

I **have to** go now or I will miss my train.
We **have to** be at school at 8.30 a.m.
You **have to** be quiet during the show.

Must hat nur eine Form und wird nur in der Gegenwart verwendet. Wenn **must** in der Vergangenheit benutzt werden soll, dann ist **have to** zu verwenden.

I **must** go.   I **had to** go.
James **has to** go.   James **had to** go.

Zwei weitere Modalverben, die zu 'müssen' gehören, sind **should** und **ought to.** Sie bedeuten ‚sollten' oder ‚eigentlich müssen'.

He said we **should** get together next week.
We **ought to** stay by the cash desk all the time.

Etwas ganz anderes bedeuten: **mustn´t** und **don´t have to**.

You **mustn´t** do that. It is dangerous.
Mustn´t bedeutet hier: Tue es nicht! Es ist notwendig, dass etwas nicht passiert.
You **don´t have** to do it if you are too tired.
Don´t have to bedeutet hier: Sie brauchen es nicht zu tun. Sie können es tun, aber es ist nicht erforderlich. Sie können in diesem Beispiel auch **needn´t** verwenden.

You **needn´t** do it if you are too tired.

Task 30

Insert **must/have to /should/ought to.**

1. You..................... try this cake. It´s delicious.
2. We...................... be in at 8 a.m.
3. First, we...................... check the building.
4. The manager said that we..................... pay more attention to the customers.
5. It is late, the baby.................... be in bed by now.
6. We .... count the money before we go home.
7. Madam, you................ try this bathfoam. It is very soft for your skin.
8. Mrs. Wembly said that we..................... change places.
9. If you want more customers, you........................ attract their attention.
10. We.................... have been home tonight, however, we went to friends.

b Erlaubnis / Einwilligung

Wenn man seine Erlaubnis *geben* will, dann verwendet man im Englischen: **can, could** oder **may.**

You **can** have a day off next week.
You **may** use a dictionary during the exams.
We **could** use a dictionary if we asked for it.

May hört sich verglichen mit **can** sehr vornehm an und wird vorwiegend in formalen Situationen verwendet. Normalerweise verwendet man **can.**

Für die Vergangenheit verwendet man **could.**
Für alle Zeiten kann man dagegen **to be allowed to** verwenden.

He will **not be allowed** to play football next Sunday.
Dogs **are not allowed** in shops!

Wenn man um Erlaubnis *bitten* will, dann können **can, could, may** und manchmal **would like** verwendet werden.

Can I ask you a question?
Can I use your lighter?

Möchte man jemanden um etwas bitten, wird üblicherweise **can** verwendet.
Could ist die höflichere Variante.

Excuse me, **could** I ask you a question?
Could you give me advice about this?

Besonders höflich klingt es gerade in formalen Situationen, wenn man **may** verwendet.

May we offer you this sample, Madam?
May we ask you some questions?
May I ask you where you bought this?

Sie können auch **would like** verwenden. Dies gilt vor allem für die Briefkorrespondenz.

We **would like to** receive information about your products.
I **would like** you **to** send me your invoice.

147

Task 31

Insert **can/could/may/would like**:

1. .... you park your car elsewhere, Sir?
2. .... we ask you where you come from?
3. We................... use the car today.
4. Howard,.................... I borrow your bike this afternoon?
5. Yes, of course. You................... use it any time this afternoon.
6. .... you tell me the time, please?
7. They told us that we....................... collect the goods.
8. We........................ to know your name.
9. The regulations make it clear that we.................. let you in.
10. .... I have another cup of tea, Mum?

c Möglichkeit

Um Möglichkeiten zu beschreiben, werden die Hilfsverben **may, might** und **could** verwendet.

Bridget **may** get promotion and be head-of-sales of her department.
Take care! The children **might** fall into the water.
We **could** go to the cinema or rent a videotape.

In vielen Fällen macht es nicht viel aus, welches Modalverb Sie verwenden.

There´s someone at the door, it **might/may/could** be Joan.

Der Unterschied zwischen **may** und **might** ist noch etwas subtiler: Bei der Verwendung von **might** ist man etwas weniger sicher, als wenn man **may** verwendet.

If I had the money, I **might** buy a red Ferrari.

Da Sie das Geld für einen Ferrari nicht haben, ist es eher unwahrscheinlich, dass Sie sich je diesen Wagen kaufen werden. In diesem Satz würde man daher kein **may** verwenden.

Task 32

Insert **may, might** or **could.** There is more than one answer.

1. She has lost her keys, they.................. be under the car.
2. You could ask the shop assistant. She .... be able to help you.
3. Don´t count on John, he....................... not come tonight.
4. I´m not sure what to buy. I..................... buy the purple vacuum cleaner.
5. We don't have it now, but we .... have it next year.
6. When I am old, I.................... go to Spain for a year.
7. If I were rich I......................... buy an Island.
8. Where can I find the manager? You .... try the second floor.
9. We .... go to the South next year.
10. I can´t find that key, we .... not have it.

d Fähigkeit

Etwas können oder **zu etwas fähig sein** übersetzt man meistens mit **can.**

I **can** play the piano.
Ich kann Klavier spielen.

In der Vergangenheit verwendet man **could.**

I **could** play well, when I practised a lot.
Ich konnte gut spielen, als ich mehr übte.

Für alle andere Formen ist **to be able to** zu verwenden.

Task 33

Bitte tragen Sie **can, could or to be able to** ein. Es sind mehrere Antworten möglich.

1. We .... order the goods for you.
2. They thought they......................... stay open till 7 p.m
3. I......................... not find the lift so I used the stairs.
4. What......................... I do for you?
5. I hope I .... help you.
6. A computer is .... store information very fast.
7. You...................... walk or take the elevator.
8. If you like the food you....................... find the recipe in the cookery book.
9. I would help you if I.........................
10. We won´t .... go there again.

149

12 Unregelmässige Verben

Lernen Sie diese auswendig!

Infinitiv	Vergangenheit	Partizip Perfekt*	Deutsch
to be	was/were	been	sein
to bear	bore	borne	tragen
to beat	beat	beaten	schlagen
to become	became	become	werden
to begin	began	begun	anfangen
to bend	bent	bent	biegen
to bet	bet	bet	wetten
to bind	bound	bound	binden
to bite	bit	bitten	beißen
to bleed	bled	bled	bluten
to blow	blew	blown	blasen
to break	broke	broken	brechen
to bring	brought	brought	bringen
to build	built	built	bauen
to burn	burnt	burnt	brennen
to burst	burst	burst	barsten
to buy	bought	bought	kaufen
to catch	caught	caught	fangen
to choose	chose	chosen	wählen
to come	came	come	kommen
to cost	cost	cost	kosten
to cut	cut	cut	schneiden
to deal	dealt	dealt	handeln
to do	did	done	tun, machen
to draw	drew	drawn	ziehen
to drink	drank	drunk	trinken
to drive	drove	driven	fahren
to eat	ate	eaten	essen
to fall	fell	fallen	fallen
to feed	fed	fed	füttern
to feel	felt	felt	fühlen
to fight	fought	fought	kämpfen
to find	found	found	finden
to flee	fled	fled	flüchten
to fly	flew	flown	fliegen
to forbid	forbade	forbidden	verbieten
to forget	forgot	forgotten	vergessen
to freeze	froze	frozen	frieren
to get	got	got	bekommen, holen
to give	gave	given	geben
to go	went	gone	gehen
to grow	grew	grown	wachsen
to hang	hung	hung	hängen
to have	had	had	haben
to hear	heard	heard	hören

to hide	hid	hidden	verstecken
to hit	hit	hit	schlagen
to hold	held	held	halten
to hurt	hurt	hurt	verletzen
to keep	kept	kept	(be)halten, aufbewahren
to know	knew	known	wissen
to lay	laid	laid	legen
to lead	led	led	führen
to leave	left	left	verlassen
to lend	lent	lent	leihen
to let	let	let	lassen
to lie	lay	lain	liegen
to light	lit	lit	anzünden
to loose	lost	lost	verlieren
to make	made	made	machen
to mean	meant	meant	meinen
to meet	met	met	begegnen
to pay	paid	paid	bezahlen
to put	put	put	legen, stellen, setzen
to read	read	read	lesen
to ring	rang	rung	klingeln
to rise	rose	risen	aufstehen
to run	ran	run	rennen
to say	said	said	sagen
to see	saw	seen	sehen
to sell	sold	sold	verkaufen
to send	sent	sent	senden
to sew	sewed	sewn/sewed	nähen
to shake	shook	shaken	schütteln
to shine	shone	shone	scheinen (Sonne)
to shoot	shot	shot	schießen
to show	showed	shown	zeigen
to shrink	shrank	shrunk	schrumpfen
to shut	shut	shut	schließen
to sing	sang	sung	singen
to sit	sat	sat	sitzen
to sleep	slept	slept	schlafen
to speak	spoke	spoken	sprechen
to spend	spent	spent	spenden
to split	split	split	reisen, barsten
to spread	spread	spread	verstreuen
to stand	stood	stood	stehen
to steal	stole	stolen	stehlen
to stick	stuck	stuck	festsitzen
to sting	stung	stung	stechen
to strike	struck	struck	schlagen
to sweep	swept	swept	fegen
to swim	swam	swum	schwimmen
to take	took	taken	nehmen
to teach	taught	taught	lehren

to tear	tore	torn	reißen
to tell	told	told	erzählen
to think	thought	thought	denken
to throw	threw	thrown	werfen
to understand	understood	understood	verstehen
to wake	woke	woken	wecken
to wear	wore	worn	tragen
to win	won	won	gewinnen
to write	wrote	written	schreiben

*Das Partizip Perfekt wird in Englisch mit 'to have' verwendet. Beispiel:
I have begun studying Englisch.
Ich habe begonnen, Englisch zu studieren.

13   Vokabeln

Lernen Sie diese auswendig!

Englisch	Deutsch
abbreviation	Abkürzung
access	Zugang
access control	Zugangskontrolle
accidentally	versehentlich
account	Bericht
accounting system	Buchführungs-, Abrechnungssystem
administration	Verwaltung
admission	Zugang
advance	Fortschritt
afternoon	Nachmittag
age	Alter
agent	Mittel
aim	Ziel
to aim	zielen
airline	Fluggesellschaft
airplane	Flugzeug
airport	Flughafen
aisle	Gang
to allocate	zuweisen
aluminium	Aluminium
a.m.	vormittags
amendment	Veränderung
ancillary facilities	Nebeneinrichtungen
annoyance	Ärger
answering machine	Anrufbeantworter
applicant	Bewerber
to appoint	einsetzen
appointment	Verabredung
to approach	sich nähern, ansprechen
appropriate	geeignet
armed forces	Streitkräfte
army	Armee
articles	Artikel
as a whole	vollständig
assembly area	Sammelstelle
to assess	einordnen
assignment	Auftrag
asterisk	Sternchen
at intervals	manchmal
at least	mindestens
atmosphere	Atmosphäre
to attend	teilnehmen
to attend to	sorgen für
attention (attn.)	Betreff (z. Hd.)
authority	Befugnis, Befehlsgewalt
available	erhältlich
to avoid	vermeiden
backed by	unterstützt durch
badge	Namensschild
bag	Tasche
baggage	Gepäck
to ban	verweisen
banner	Transparent
banning	Verbot
barrier	Schlagbaum
base	Stützpunkt
basement	Untergeschoss
bathroom	Badezimmer
to be able to	können
to be addressed	angesprochen werden
to be caught	gefasst werden
to be committed to	verpflichtet sein
to be embarrassed	verlegen sein
to beep	piepsen, ein akkustisches Signal geben
to be entitled	berechtigt sein
to believe	glauben
belongings	Wertsachen
belt	Gürtel
to be managed	verwaltet werden
to be mistaken	im Irrtum sein
to be obliged to	verpflichtet sein zu etw.
to be on duty	Dienst haben
to be on surveillance	patrouillieren, einen Rundgang machen

Englisch	Deutsch
to be spoken to	angesprochen werden
to be torn apart	auseinander gerissen werden
beverage	Getränk
bill	Rechnung
blank	unausgefüllt
to bolt	verschrauben
bottle	Flasche
branch office	Filiale
brandy	Kognak
breach	Verstoß, Übertretung
breakfast	Frühstück
brittle	zerbrechlich
building site	Baustelle
bulk luggage	Reisegepäck
bulky	sperrig
button	Knopf
by fits and starts	in Intervallen
by radio	über Funk
to call	anrufen
calm	ruhig
can	Dose
cancellation	Absage
canteen	Kantine
car park	Parkplatz
case	Fall
cash desk	Kasse
to catch out	hereinlegen
caustic	ätzend
CCTV	Kameraüberwachung
central station	Hauptbahnhof
to check	kontrollieren
chemist's	Drogerie
choice	Wahl
church road	Kirchstraße
citizen	Bürger
client	Kunde
coin	Münze
colleague	Kollegin/ Kollege
to collect	abholen
to come in handy	gut gebrauchen können
to commence	beginnen
to commision	berechnen
to commit	begehen
commitment	Verpflichtung
community service	sozialer Dienst
company	Firma
complicated	schwierig
to comply with	entsprechen, etw. erfüllen
computer centre	Rechenzentrum
conduct	Vorgehen
to confess	gestehen, zugeben
to confirm	bestätigen
confirmation	Bestätigung
continental	kontinental, europäisch
continuing	ständig
contract	Vertrag
control centre	Leitstelle
controller	Fachkraft für Notruf- serviceleitstelle
conversation	Gespräch
conveyor belt	Fließband
to connect	verbinden
cord	Schnur, Band
corridor	Gang
cost effective	kostensparend
to count	zählen
counter	Tresen
covert	versteckt
cram-full	überfüllt
to create	kreieren, gestalten, bilden
crisps	Chips
crossroads	Kreuzung
curious	neugierig
current	aktuell, jüngste/r

153

currently	gerade
customer	Kunde
daily	täglich
to damage	beschädigen
danger	Gefahr
to deal	behandeln
decent	anständig
decision	Entscheidung
definitely	bestimmt
to defy	hinwegsetzen
demand	Forderung
department	Abteilung
department store	Kaufhaus
to design	entwerfen
detached to	angeschlossen
to detain	festhalten
detention centre	Jugendstrafanstalt
to develop	entwickeln
device	Gerät
dialogue	Dialog
difference	Unterschied
to direct	leiten, anweisen
direction	Richtung
to disappoint	enttäuschen
to discharge	entladen
to discourage	abschrecken, entmutigen
dispatch	Versand
display cabinet	Schaukasten
disposal	Abfallentsorgung / Verfügung
to dispose of	entsorgen
distance	Entfernung
to distinguish	unterscheiden
domiciliary right	Hausrecht
Do you have a light?	Haben Sie Feuer?
to draw	zeichnen
due to	mit Dank an
dyestuff	Färbemittel
effort	Mühe
to eject	verweisen
electronic article surveillance	elektronische Artikelüberwachung
electronic tag	Diebstahlsicherung, Schild
elevator	Aufzug, Fahrstuhl
to eliminate	ausschließen
elusive	schwer zu fangen
emperor	Kaiser
emergency phone	Notruftelefon
to empty	leeren
to enable	ermöglichen
to encounter	antreffen
endangered	gefährdet
engaged	besetzt
to enquire	sich erkundigen
to enter	betreten
entitlement	Berechtigung
entrance	Eingang
entry ticket	Eintrittskarte
to equip	ausrüsten, ausstatten
equipment	Ausrüstung
error	Fehler
essential	wesentlich
evacuation plan	Rettungsplan
evacuation scheme	Rettungsplan
event	Veranstaltung, Ereignis
to examine	untersuchen
example	Beispiel
to exchange	austauschen
exercise	Übung
to exercise	ausüben
exhibition	Ausstellung
exit	Ausgang
exit graphic	Rettungsschild
experience	Erfahrung
expertise	Fachkenntnis
expression	Ausdruck
extension	Nebenanschluss, Apparat, Durchwahl
extensive	umfangreich
eyewitness	Augenzeuge
facility	Einrichtung
to faint	ohnmächtig werden
fair	Messe
family name	Nachname
featured	abgebildet
federal police	Bundespolizei
to feel comfortable	sich wohl fühlen
to fight	bekämpfen
to file a complaint	Beschwerde einreichen
file	Datei
filing	Archivieren
fine	Buß-, Verwarnungsgeld, Geldstrafe
fire brigade	Feuerwehr
fire department	Feuerwehr
fire detector	Brandmelder
fire doors	Brandschutztüren
fire exit	Notausgang
fire extinguisher	Feuerlöscher
fire-fighting facilities	Löscheinrichtungen
fire-fighting equipment	Löscheinrichtungen
fire hose	Feuerlöschschlauch
fire prevention training	Brandschutzlehrgang
fireworks	Feuerwerk
first name	Vorname
flare	Fackel
flame detector	Brandmelder
flame root	Flammenkern
floor	Etage, Stockwerk
flow chart	Flussdiagramm
focussing on	richten auf
folder	Ordner
to force	zwingen
to forget	vergessen
to format	formatieren
from abroad	aus dem Ausland
full board	Vollpension
fur	Pelz
gate detector	Torsonde
to gather	sammeln, zusammenpacken
gents	Herrentoilette
to get downtown	in die (Innen-) stadt kommen
to get s. b. wrong	jmd. falsch verstehen
gift	Geschenk
glad	froh
goods	Güter, Waren
to grant	gestatten
ground floor	Parterre
ground plan	Geländeplan
guard	Wachposten
guilty	schuldig
gun	Waffe
hairdresser's	Friseursalon
hand detector	Handsonde
handle	Griff
hand luggage	Handgepäck
hand-picked	sorgfältig ausgewählt
to happen	passieren, ereignen
to harass	belästigen
hard evidence	klare Beweise
to have	haben
to have to	müssen
to have two weeks off	zwei Wochen frei haben
hawk	Falke
to hide	verstecken
to highlight	hervorheben, mit Leuchtstift markieren
highly advanced	fortgeschritten
to hire	einstellen
hole	Loch
holiday	Ferien
honest	ehrlich
ID card	Personalausweis
i. e.	d. h.
ill	krank
in advance	im voraus
to indicate	anzeigen, -deuten
to injure	verletzen
indisputable	unstrittig
innovation	Innovation
in one step	in einem Schritt
in possession of	in Besitz von
instruction	Anweisung
to interfere	behindern
interference	Störung
introduction	Einleitung
intruder	Eindringling

investment	Investition
invitation	Einladung
to involve	einbeziehen, mit sich bringen
issue	Angelegenheit
item	Gegenstand
jaybird	Eichelhäher
job	Arbeit, Stelle
to joke	scherzen
to keep clear	frei halten
to keep in mind	nicht vergessen
to keep up to date	auf dem neuesten Stand bleiben
key holding service	Schlüsselverwaltung
keyword	Schlüsselwort
kind	Art, Sorte
knife	Messer
to know	wissen
lad	Typ
large-scale contract	Großauftrag
last name	Nachname
to learn by heart	auswendig lernen
to leave	verlassen
letter of application	Bewerbungsschreiben
litter-bin	Abfalleimer
liquid	flüssig
location	Ort
to look forward to	sich freuen auf
to look like	aussehen wie
loss prevention	Schadenverhütung
low key support	Schließdienst
luggage	Gepäck
madam	gnädige Frau
magazine	Zeitschrift
main entrance	Haupteingang
main road	Hauptstraße
main station	Hauptbahnhof
to maintain	führen
to make a fuss	Aufheben um etwas machen
to make notes	Notizen machen
male	männlich
manager	Manager, Betriebsleiter, Abteilungsleiter
manual	per Hand, manuell
map	Geländeplan
marine	Marinesoldat
market	Markt
marvellous	großartig
mature	reif
means	Mittel
measures	Maßnahmen
meeting	Besprechung, Konferenz
meeting point	Treffpunkt
memo	Mitteilung, Notiz
to memorize	auswendig lernen
to mention	erwähnen
message	Nachricht
metal detection gate	Torsonde
metal detector	Torsonde
mirror	Spiegel
mistake	Fehler
mix-up	Verwechslung
to monitor	überwachen
mobile (phone)	Handy
mostly	meistens
multi-layered	vielschichtig
nailscissors	Nagelschere
national requirements	nationale Anforderungen
national standards	nationale Anforderungen
nationwide	national
to neglect	vernachlässigen
New Year's Eve	Silvesterabend
(news) paper	Zeitung
no longer	nicht mehr
note	Anmerkung, Vermerk
to note	zur Kenntnis nehmen
to notify	melden
number	Zahl
a number of	eine Anzahl
observance of	Beobachtung von

to observe	beobachten
obstacle	Hindernis
obstruction	Hindernis
occasion	Gelegenheit
of course	natürlich
of high profile	von hoher Qualität
offence	Straftat, Vergehen
offender	Täter, Rechtsbrecher
offer	Angebot
on behalf of	im Namen von
on request	auf Anfrage
on the spot	vor Ort
operator	Telefonist (in) / Betreiber, Inhaber
opposite	gegenüber
options	Möglichkeiten
out of reach	außer Reichweite
overtime	Überstunden
to owe	schuldig sein
packed	brechend voll
to page	ausrufen
to panic	in Panik geraten
particular	speziell
particulars	Personalien
path	Weg
to pay attention to	beachten
to pee	pinkeln
to perforate	perforieren
to perform	erfüllen
permit	Genehmigung
persistent	beharrlich
phased	in Phasen
pin	Sicherungspin
plant maintenance	Wartungsabteilung
plastic	Kunststoff
platform	Bahnsteig
pole	Stange
police department	Polizei
possession	Besitz
possibility	Möglichkeit
possibly	möglicherweise
postal code	Postleitzahl
post room	Poststelle
potentional	möglich
to practise	üben
to prefer	bevorzugen
premises	Gelände, Gebäude, Gebiet
to present	vorlegen
pressurised	druckbeaufschlagt
previous	früher
prison	Gefängnis
probation	Bewährung
production	Produktion
to prohibit	verbieten
prohibited	verboten
to pronounce	aussprechen
pronunciation	Aussprache
to provide	zur Verfügung stellen
to punch	lochen
to purchase	käuflich erwerben
purpose	Absicht, Intention
queue	Schlange
quiet	ruhig
range	Angebot
rate	Preis
razor blade	Rasierklinge
to reach	erreichen
reason	Grund
receipt	Kassenbon
to receive	empfangen
recently	kürzlich
recipe	Rezept
to recommend	empfehlen
regulations	Bestimmungen
to reject	abweisen
remote	fern
resistance	Widerstand
resource	Mittel
response	Reaktion
restricted	beschränkt
ridiculous	lächerlich
to repeat	wiederholen
report	Bericht

155

to represent	gegenwärtig sein
to require	benötigen
research department	Forschungsabteilung
to reserve seats	Plätze reservieren
responsible	verantwortungsbewusst, zuverlässig
road constructions	Straßenbauarbeiten
safe	sicher (außer Gefahr)
safety	Sicherheit
safety and security specialist	Fachkraft für Schutz und Sicherheit
sales department	Verkaufsabteilung
scene	Ort des Geschehens
screen	Bildschirm
to search	durchsuchen
season ticket	Dauerkarte
secure	sicher (vor Angriffen)
security	Sicherheit
security area	Sicherheitsbereich
security officer	Schutz- und Sicherheitskraft
sensitive	vernünftig
sentence	Urteil, Strafe, Strafmaß
service	Service, Dienst
to settle the matter	die Angelegenheit regeln
sheet	Blatt
shift work	Schichtarbeit
short	kurz
shower	Dusche
shuttle bus	Pendelbus
to sign	unterschreiben
single room	Einzelzimmer
skill	Fertigkeit, Geschick
slang	Umgangssprache
sleeve	Hülle
to smash	zerschlagen
smoking area	Raucherzone
to smudge	verschmieren
snooper	Schnüffler
sophisticated	hoch entwickelt
solid	fest
sound	Laut, Klang
to sound	klingen
to sound the alarm	Alarm schlagen
space	Raum
special incident	ein spezieller Vorfall
spot	Platz
splittering	splitternd
to squeeze	pressen, zerdrücken
stadium regulations	Stadionordnung
staff	Belegschaft, Personal
stairs	Treppe, Treppen
stairway	Treppe, Treppenhaus
stand	Stand
standard	Niveau
stand-by	auf Empfang bleiben
to stand for	bedeuten
statement	Aussage, Stellungnahme
stationery	Schreibwaren
to stay	bleiben
stewarding service	Kontrolldienst
sticker	Aufkleber
to stock	lagern
storage	Lagerung
store detective	Ladendetektiv
storeroom	Magazin
straight	direkt
straight ahead	geradeaus
strap	Riemen, Gurt
subway	U-Bahn
suddenly	plötzlich
to suit	passen
supervisor	Leiter, Aufseher
to supply	versorgen
to surrender	aushändigen
to survey	überwachen
to suspect	verdächtigen
suspended	zur Bewährung ausgesetzt
suspicious	verdächtig
Swiss army knife	Schweizer Messer
to switch off	ausschalten
to sweep	hier: bewegen
switchboard	Empfang, Zentrale
synagogue	Synagoge
to tackle	angreifen, zur Rede stellen

to tag	etikettieren, mit einem Anhänger versehen
to tailor	anpassen
to take off	ausziehen, ablegen
tall	groß
tax free	steuerfrei
task	Aufgabe
tatty	schmuddelig
tenacity	Hartnäckigkeit
terrific	großartig
to take place	stattfinden
to take turns	sich abwechseln
targeting	zum Ziel haben
T-crossing	T-Kreuzung
temptation	Versuchung
theft	Diebstahl
thief	Dieb
thrilled	begeistert
to tick	ankreuzen
ticket office	Theaterkasse
to tie up	zusammenpassen
tighter	strenger, straffer
torch	Taschenlampe
tourist office	Touristikzentrale
town	Stadt
toy	Spielzeug
to track	verfolgen
tram	Straßenbahn
to translate	übersetzen
travellers	Reisende
tray	Tablett
to trigger	auslösen
trunk call	Ferngespräch
to try	versuchen
to turn so. o. away	jmd. zurückweisen
twinbedded	mit zwei Betten
unattended	unbewacht
unbeatable	unschlagbar
underground	Untergrund
underlined	unterstrichen
up to	bis zu
to urge	eindringlich bitten
valid	gültig
valuables	Wertgegenstände, Wertsachen
various	verschiedene
venue	Tagung
verdict	Urteil
video surveillance	Videoüberwachung
vigilance	Wachsamkeit
village	Dorf
visitor	Besucher
vital to	entscheidend
to wait	warten
Wait and see!	Nur abwarten!
waiting list	Warteliste
wallet	Brieftasche
warning	Verwarnung, Warnung
waste	Abfall
way of saying	Ausdrucksweise
to wear	tragen
well-to-do	reich
wheelchair	Rollstuhl
will	wird
to wind up	abschließen
wire	Draht
without	ohne
to witness	bezeugen, mit ansehen
to wonder	sich fragen
workshop	Werkstatt
worth	im Wert von
would-be	potentiell
would like to	würde gerne
xenophobic	fremden-, ausländerfeindlich
X-ray machine	Röntgengerät
X-ray radiation	Röntgenstrahlung
Abfall	waste

Lernen Sie diese auswendig!

Deutsch	Englisch
Abfalleimer	litter-bin
Abfallentsorgung	disposal
Abgebildet	featured
abholen	to collect
ablegen	to take off
Abteilung	department
Absage	cancellation
abschließen	to wind up
abschrecken, entmutigen	to discourage
Absicht, Intention	purpose
abweisen	to reject
aktuell, jüngste/r	current
Alarm schlagen	to sound the alarm
Alter	age
Aluminium	aluminium
Angebot	offer
Angelegenheit	issue
angesprochen werden	to be addressed
angeschlossen	detached to
angesprochen werden	to be spoken to
angreifen, zur Rede stellen	to tackle
ankreuzen	to tick
Anlass, Gelegenheit	occasion
Anmerkung, Vermerk	note
anpassen	to tailor
Anrufbeantworter	answering machine
anrufen	to call
ansprechen	to approach
anständig	decent
antreffen	to encounter
Anweisung	instruction
anweisen	to direct
anzeigen, -deuten	to indicate
Arbeit, Stelle	job
Archivieren	filing
Ärger	annoyance
Armee	army
Art, Sorte	kind
Artikel	articles
Atmosphäre	atmosphere
ätzend	caustic
auf Anfrage	on request
auf dem neuesten Stand bleiben	to keep up to date
auf Empfang bleiben	stand-by
Aufgabe	task
Aufheben um etw. machen	to make a fuss
Aufkleber	sticker
Auftrag	assignment
Aufzug	elevator
Augenzeuge	eyewitness
aus dem Ausland	from abroad
Ausdruck	expression
Ausdrucksweise	way of saying
Ausgang	exit
aushändigen	to surrender
auseinander gerissen werden	to be torn apart
auslösen	to trigger
ausrüsten, ausstatten	to equip
ausrufen	to page
Aussage, Stellungnahme	statement
ausschalten	to switch off
ausschließen	to eliminate
aussehen wie	to look like
außer Reichweite	out of reach
Aussprache	pronunciation
aussprechen	to pronounce
Ausstellung	exhibition
Ausrüstung	equipment
ausüben	to exercise
austauschen	to exchange
auswendig lernen	to learn by heart, to memorize
ausziehen	to take off
Badezimmer	bathroom
Bahnsteig	platform
Baustelle	building site
beachten	to pay attention to
bedeuten	to stand for
Befugnis, Befehlsgewalt	authority
begehen	to commit
begeistert	thrilled
beginnen	to commence
behandeln	to deal
beharrlich	persistent
behindern	to interfere
Beispiel	example
bekämpfen	to fight
belästigen	to harass
Belegschaft, Personal	staff
Beobachtung von	observance of
benötigen	to require
beobachten	to observe
berechnen	to commision
Berechtigung	entitlement
berechtigt sein	to be entitled
Bericht	account, report
beschädigen	to damage
beschränkt	restricted
Beschwerde einreichen	to file a complaint
besetzt	engaged
Besitz	possession
Besprechung, Konferenz	meeting
bestätigen	to confirm
bestimmt	definitely
Bestimmungen	regulations
Besucher	visitor
Betreff (z. Hd.)	attention (attn.)
Betreiber, Inhaber	operator
betreten	to enter
bevorzugen	to prefer
Bewährung	probation
bewegen	to sweep
Bewerber	applicant
Bewerbungsschreiben	letter of application
bezeugen, mit ansehen	to witness
bilden	to create
Bildschirm	screen
bis	up to
Blatt	sheet
bleiben	to stay
Brandmelder	fire detector, flame detector
Brandschutzlehrgang	fire prevention training
Brandschutztüren	fire doors
brechend voll	packed
Brieftasche	wallet
Buchführungs-, Abrech-nungssystem	accounting system
Bürger	citizen
Bundespolizei	federal police
Buß-, Verwarnungsgeld, Geldstrafe	fine
Chips	crisps
Datei	file
Dauerkarte	season ticket
d. h.	i. e.
Dialog	dialogue
die Angelegenheit regeln	to settle the matter
Dieb	thief
Diebstahl	theft
Diebstahlsicherung, Schild	electronic tag
Dienst haben	to be on duty
direkt	straight
Dorf	village
Dose	can
Draht	wire
Drogerie	chemist's
druckbeaufschlagt	pressurized
durchsuchen	to search
Durchwahl	extension
Dusche	shower
ehrlich	honest
Eichelhäher	jaybird
eindringlich bitten	to urge
Eindringling	intruder
eine Anzahl von	a number of
Eingang	entrance
Einladung	invitation
Einleitung	introduction
einordnen	to assess
Einrichtung	facility

157

einsetzen	to appoint	Genehmigung	permit
einstellen	to hire	Gepäck	luggage, baggage
Eintrittskarte	entry ticket	Gerade	currently
Einzelzimmer	single room	geradeaus	straight ahead
elektronische Artikelüber-	electronic article	Gerät	device
wachung	surveillance	Geschenk	gift
Empfang, Zentrale	switchboard	Gespräch	conversation
empfangen	to receive	gestatten	to grant
empfehlen	to recommend	gestehen, zugeben	to confess
Entfernung	distance	Getränk	beverage
entladen	to discharge	glauben	to believe
entscheidend	vital to	Gnädige Frau	madam
entsorgen	to dispose of	Griff	handle
entsprechen, etw. erfüllen	to comply with	groß	tall
enttäuschen	to disappoint	großartig	marvellous, terrific
Erfahrung	experience	Großauftrag	large-scale contract
erhältlich	available	Grund	reason
einbeziehen, mit sich	to involve	gültig	valid
bringen		Gürtel	belt
Entscheidung	decision	Güter, Waren	goods
entwerfen	to design	gut gebrauchen können	to come in handy
entwickeln	to develop		
erfüllen	to perform	haben	to have
ermöglichen	to enable	Haben Sie Feuer?	Do you have a light?
erreichen	to reach	Handgepäck	hand luggage
erwähnen	to mention	Handsonde	hand detector
Etage, Stockwerk	floor	Handy	mobile (phone)
etikettieren, mit einem	to tag	Hartnäckigkeit	tenacity
Anhänger versehen		Hauptbahnhof	main station, central station
		Haupteingang	main entrance
Färbemittel	dyestuff	Hauptstraße	main road
Fachkenntnis	expertise	Hausrecht	domiciliary right
Fachkraft für Schutz und	safety and security	hereinlegen	to catch out
Sicherheit	specialist	Herrentoilette	gents
Fachkraft für Notruf-	controller	hervorheben, mit Leucht-	to highlight
serviceleitstelle		stift markieren	
Fackel	flare	Hindernis	obstacle
Fahrstuhl	elevator	hinwegsetzen	to defy
Falke	hawk	hoch entwickelt	sophisticated
Fall	case	Hülle	sleeve
Fehler	mistake, error		
Ferien	holiday	im Irrtum sein	to be mistaken
fern	remote	im Namen von	on behalf of
Ferngespräch	trunk call	im voraus	in advance
Fertigkeit, Geschick	skill	im Wert von	worth
fest	solid	in Besitz von	in possession of
festhalten	to detain	in die (Innen-) stadt	to get downtown
Feuerlöscher	fire extinguisher	kommen	
Feuerlöschschlauch	fire hose	in einem Schritt	in one step
Feuerwehr	fire department, fire brigade	in Intervallen	by fits and starts
Feuerwerk	fireworks	Innovation	innovation
Filiale	branch office	in Phasen	phased
Firma	company	Investition	investment
Flammenkern	flame root		
Flasche	bottle	jmd. falsch verstehen	to get s. b. wrong
Fließband	conveyor belt	jmd. zurückweisen	to turn s.o. away
Fluggesellschaft	airline	Jugendstrafanstalt	detention centre
Flughafen	airport		
Flugzeug	airplane	Kaiser	emperor
Flussdiagramm	flow chart	Kameraüberwachung	CCTV
flüssig	liquid	Kantine	canteen
Forderung	demand	Kasse	cash desk
Forschungsabteilung	research department	Kassenbon	receipt
Fortgeschritten	highly advanced	Kaufhaus	department store
formatieren	to format	käuflich erwerben	to purchase
Fortschritt	advance	Kirchstraße	church road
frei halten	to keep clear	klare Beweise	hard evidence
Fremden-, ausländer-	xenophobic	klingen	to sound
feindlich		Knopf	button
Friseursalon	hairdresser's	können	to be able to
froh	glad	Kognak	brandy
früher, vorherig	previous	Kontrolldienst	stewarding service
Frühstück	breakfast	Kollege/ Kollegin	colleague
führen	to maintain	kontinental, europäisch	continental
		kontrollieren	to check
Gang	corridor, aisle	Kosten sparend	cost effective
geeignet	appropriate	krank	ill
Gefahr	danger	kreieren, gestalten	to create
gefährdet	endangered	Kreuzung	crossroads
Gefängnis	prison	Kunde	client, customer
gefasst werden	to be caught	Kunststoff	plastic
Gegenstand	item	kurz	short
gegenüber	opposite	kürzlich	recently
gegenwärtig sein	to represent		
Gelände, Gebäude	premises	lächerlich	ridiculous
Geländeplan	map, ground plan	Ladendetektiv	store detective

lagern	to stock
Lagerung	storage
Laut, Klang	sound
leeren	to empty
leiten	to direct
Leiter, Aufseher	supervisor
Leitstelle	control centre
Loch	hole
lochen	to punch
Löscheinrichtungen	fire-fighting equipment, fire-fighting facilities
Magazin	storeroom
männlich	male
Manager, Betriebs-, Abteilungsleiter	manager
manchmal	at intervals
Maßnahmen	measures
Marinesoldat	marine
Markt	market
meistens	mostly
melden	to notify
Messe	fair
Messer	knife
mindestens	at least
mit Dank an	due to
Mitteilung, Notiz	memo
Mittel	means / resource
Mittel	agent
mit zwei Betten	twinbedded
möglich	potentional
Möglichkeit	possibility, option
möglicherweise	possibly
Mühe	effort
Münze	coin
müssen	to have to
Nachmittag	afternoon
Nachname	family name
Nachname	last name
Nachricht	message
Nagelschere	nailscissors
Namensschild	badge
national	nationwide
nationale Anforderungen	national requirements, national standards
natürlich	of course
Nebenanschluss, Apparat	extension
Nebeneinrichtungen	ancillary facilities
neugierig	curious
nicht mehr	no longer
nicht vergessen	to keep in mind
Niveau	standard
Notausgang	fire exit
Notizen machen	to make notes
Notruftelefon	emergency phone
Nur abwarten!	Wait and see!
ohne	without
ohnmächtig werden	to faint
Ordner	folder
Ort	location
Ort des Geschehens	scene
in Panik geraten	to panic
Parkplatz	car park
Parterre	ground floor
passen	to suit
passieren, ereignen	to happen
patrouillieren, einen Rundgang machen	to be on surveillance
Pelz	fur
Pendelbus	shuttle bus
perforieren	to perforate
per Hand, manuell	manual
Personalausweis	ID card
Personalien	particulars
piepsen, ein akkustisches Signal geben	to beep
pinkeln	to pee
Platz	spot
Plätze reservieren	to reserve seats
plötzlich	suddenly
Polizei	police department
Postleitzahl	postal code
Poststelle	post room

potentiell	would-be
Preis	rate
pressen, drücken	to squeeze
Produktion	production
Rasierklinge	razor blade
Raucherzone	smoking area
Raum	space
Reaktion	response
Rechenzentrum	computer centre
Rechnung	bill
reich	well-to-do
reif	mature
Reisegepäck	bulk luggage
Reisende	travellers
Rettungsplan	evacuation scheme, evacuation plan
Rettungsschild	exit graphic
Rezept	recipe
richten auf	focussing on
Richtung	direction
Riemen, Gurt	strap
Röntgengerät	X-ray machine
Röntgenstrahlung	X-ray radiation
Rollstuhl	wheelchair
ruhig	quiet, calm
sammeln	to gather
Sammelstelle	assembly area
Schadenverhütung	loss prevention
Schaukasten	display cabinet
scherzen	to joke
Schicht, Überzug	coating
Schichtarbeit	shiftwork
Schnur, Band	cord
Schlagbaum	barrier
Schlange	queue
Schließdienst	low key support
Schlüsselverwaltung	key holding service
Schlüsselwort	keyword
schmuddelig	tatty
Schnüffler	snooper
Schreibwaren	stationery
schuldig	guilty
schuldig sein	to owe
Schutz- und Sicherheits- kraft	security officer
Schweizer Messer	Swiss army knife
schwer zu fangen	elusive
schwierig	complicated
Service, Dienst	service
sich abwechseln	to take turns
sicher (außer Gefahr)	safe
sicher (vor Angriffen)	secure
Sicherheit	security
Sicherheit	safety
Sicherheitsbereich	security area
sich erkundigen	to enquire
Sicherungspin	pin
sich fragen	to wonder
sich freuen auf	to look forward to
sich nähern	to approach
sich wohl fühlen	to feel comfortable
Silvesterabend	New Year's Eve
sozialer Dienst	community service
sorgen für	to attend to
sorgfältig ausgewählt	hand-picked
sperrig	bulky
speziell	particular
spezieller Vorfall	special incident
Spiegel	mirror
Spielzeug	toy
splitternd	splittering
Stadionordnung	stadium regulations
Stadt	town
Stand	stand
ständig	continuing
Stange	pole
stattfinden	to take place
Sternchen	asterisk
steuerfrei	taxfree
Störung	interference
Straßenbahn	tram
Straßenbauarbeiten	road constructions
Streitkräfte	armed forces

strenger, straffer	tighter
Stützpunkt	base
Synagoge	synagogue
Tablett	tray
täglich	daily
Tagung	venue
Tasche	bag
Taschenlampe	torch
Täter, Rechtsbrecher	offender
teilnehmen	to attend
Telefonist (in)	operator
Theaterkasse	ticket office
T-Kreuzung	T-crossing
Torsonde	metal detection gate, gate detector, metal detector
Touristikzentrale	tourist office
tragen	to wear
Transparent	banner
Treffpunkt	meeting point
Treppe	stairs, stairway
Treppenhaus	stairway
Tresen	counter
Typ	lad
U-Bahn	subway
üben	to practise
überfüllt	cram-full
über Funk	by radio
übersetzen	to translate
Überstunden	overtime
überwachen	to monitor, to survey
Übung	exercise
umfangreich	extensive
Umgangssprache	slang
unausgefüllt	blank
unbewacht	unattended
unschlagbar	unbeatable
unstrittig	indisputable
Untergeschoss	basement
Untergrund	underground
Unterscheiden	to distinguish
Unterschied	difference
unterschreiben	to sign
unterstrichen	underlined
unterstützt durch	backed by
untersuchen	to examine
Urteil, Strafe, Strafmaß	sentence
Urteil	verdict
Verabredung	appointment
Veränderung	amendment
Veranstaltung, Ereignis	event
verantwortungsbewusst, zuverlässig	responsible
verbieten	to prohibit
verbinden	to connect
Verbot	banning
verboten	prohibited
verdächtig	suspicious
verdächtigen	to suspect
verfolgen	to track
Verfügung	disposal
Vergehen, Straftat	offence
vergessen	to forget
Verkaufsabteilung	sales department
verlassen	to leave
verlegen sein	to be embarrassed
verletzen	to injure
vermeiden	to avoid
vernachlässigen	to neglect
vernünftig	sensitive
verpflichtet sein zu etw.	to be obliged to, to be committed to
Verpflichtung	commitment
Versand	dispatch
verschiedene	various
verschmieren	to smudge
verschrauben	to bolt
versehentlich	accidentally
versorgen	to supply
verstecken	to hide
versteckt	covert
Verstoß, Übertretung	breach
versuchen	to try

Versuchung	temptation
Vertrag	contract
verwaltet werden	to be managed
Verwaltung	administration
Verwarnung, Warnung	warning
Verwechslung	mix-up
verweisen	to eject, to ban
Videoüberwachung	camera surveillance
vielschichtig	multi-layered
Vollpension	full board
vollständig	as a whole
von hoher Qualität	of high profile
vorgehen	conduct
vorlegen	to present
vormittags	a.m.
vor Ort	on the spot
Vorname	first name
Wachposten	guard
Wachsamkeit	vigilance
Waffe	gun
Wahl	choice
Warteliste	waiting list
warten	to wait
Wartungsabteilung	plant maintenance
Weg	path
Werkstatt	workshop
Wertgegenstände, Wertsachen	valuables
Wertsachen	belongings
wesentlich	essential
Widerstand	resistance
wiederholen	to repeat
wissen	to know
wird	will
würde gerne	would like to
Zahl	number
zählen	to count
zeichnen	to draw
Zeitschrift	magazine
Zeitung	(news) paper
zerbrechlich	brittle
zerschlagen	to smash
Ziel	aim
zielen	to aim
Zugang	access, admission
Zugangskontrolle	access control
zum Ziel haben	targeting
zur Bewährung ausgesetzt	suspended
zur Kenntnis nehmen	to note
zur Verfügung stellen	to provide
zusammenpacken	to gather
zusammenpassen	to tie up
zuweisen	to allocate
zwei Wochen frei haben	to have two weeks off
zwingen	to force